Advance Praise

"Insanely inspiring . . . beautifully simple . . . masterfully told. In times past, Stephen Covey rocked the business world with his *Seven Habits* bestseller. For a new generation, Steve Rigby ignites ours with his Six Keys that unlock the doors to *self*-management—a human longing as *old* as time."

—Chris Sarbora, Distinguished Engineer for General Motors; Thirteen-Time Isle of Man TT Racer and Record-Holder

"Steve Rigby has a rare gift for turning leadership into something practical, relatable, and real. *Managing* to S.M.I.L.E. shows how to develop *self*-managed people who are empowered to take ownership, grow in confidence, and rise to their full potential. This isn't just a book; it's a roadmap for developing people who believe in themselves and the impact they can make."

—Harry Roberts, Cofounder of Mattress Firm

"*Managing* to S.M.I.L.E. is a smart, uplifting guide that shows leaders how to empower their teams while improving their own quality of life. It blends practical leadership insight with a focus on health, balance, and personal responsibility. The *Self*-Management Model is especially powerful and has already made a real difference for early readers. This book offers clear, meaningful tools for creating positive change at work and at home."

—David Osborn, Founder of Gobundance; Real Estate Investor and Entrepreneur; *NYT* Best-Selling Author of *Wealth Can't Wait*

"*Managing* to S.M.I.L.E. is a masterclass in leadership and a blueprint for freedom. Through powerful stories and timeless lessons, it shows how real success begins with *self*-management and expands through empowering others. This book reminds us that great leaders don't pull strings—they cut them, creating space for people to grow, rise up, and smile! It's practical, heartfelt, and packed with wisdom for anyone who wants to lead with purpose, elevate others, and build a life—and business—that truly smiles back."

—Jordan Adler, Author of the Amazon Bestseller, *Beach Money;* Network Marketing Entrepreneur and Multi-Million-Dollar Producer

"*Managing* to S.M.I.L.E. brings Steve Rigby's timeless sales philosophy from **S.M.I.L.E.** full circle. His follow-up book is a refreshing guide for anyone who wants to build high-performing teams by leading with trust, clarity, and genuine care. He shows us—as only Steve can—that when people are empowered, both performance *and* fulfillment follow."

—Holly James, D.R. Horton Region Vice President Southeast Texas

"As the principal in our contracting company, *Managing* to S.M.I.L.E. articulates something I see every day in leadership: people don't perform better because they're managed harder; they perform better when they understand what's expected of them and choose accountability. This book reframes leadership away from control and toward freedom, ownership, and trust—the very elements that drive consistent performance in complex real-world environments. It's a must read for any leader responsible for both results and people.

As an author myself, I find Steve's book aligns deeply with work I do around boundaries, responsibility, and personal ownership—positions we must consider as we choose who has access to the most important rooms in our lives. In my experience, lasting change only happens when accountability is chosen, not imposed, and this book captures that truth with clarity and care. *Managing* to S.M.I.L.E. is a meaningful, human-centered guide for leaders who want growth that lasts."

— Wendy Knipp, Principal, Knipp Contracting; Speaker and Author of *The Rooms in Your House*

"In his follow-on book to the best-selling **S.M.I.L.E.**, Steve Rigby offers a blueprint for empowerment, for *self*-management. *Managing* to S.M.I.L.E. is a must for every team leader and member. Even an entrepreneur or intrapreneur will find invaluable help in growing one's business and personhood. This book is a real gem. I only wish I'd had it when I was a new manager.

—Lynette Sheppard, Author of *The Everyday Enneagram, A Personality Map for Enhancing Your Work, Love, and Life . . . Everyday*

"For decades, Steve has taught the importance of making human connections over transactions. This book fills the missing link—training you to manage correctly as you enable your sales team to practice what they're learning: caring gets more closings. I'm guilty of having been a young manager who thought I was a symphony conductor—with my staff working as extensions of me. This book turns that upside down and demonstrates, in a fun way, how to truly empower your people to take ownership of how they care about customers when you're not around."

— Ken Pinto, Homebuilding Veteran; Author of *How Much Is the Milk?*

"*Managing* to S.M.I.L.E. provides a practical story-driven guide that shows you how to lead with clarity, trust, and real human connection. After seizing the benefits of *self*-management, you'll then grasp the rewards of empowering others. The consistent takeaway lies in Steve moving leadership *away* from control and micromanagement and *toward* ownership and accountability—which works!—regardless of who is or isn't in the room.

The tie-in to addiction is real because addiction is a breakdown of *self*-management where impulse, secrecy, and excuses take control. This book reinforces the opposite: values, discipline, honesty, and healthy connections. Those battling addiction will enthusiastically embrace it, as well as those trusted with treating it. And even if addiction isn't your story, the same framework applies to breaking patterns that limit performance, create stress, fuel burnout, promote procrastination, and stifle creativity. It delivers real results by giving the reader a clear model to follow to live a better, happier, and more productive life."

—Montana Harris, Owner and Founder of EZR Lives and EZR Recovery

"Steve Rigby has done it again. In **S.M.I.L.E.**, he had us pause, reflect, and redesign both our businesses and our lives with a focus on putting people and relationships first. *Managing* to S.M.I.L.E. goes deeper. Steve ingenuously builds on that foundation with warmth, insight, and practical wisdom, offering actionable steps that inspire confidence to take control of our lives.

I marvel at how his Six Keys to *self*-management beautifully align with The LITL System I created and wrote about in my book. That alignment reminds us that growth takes commitment and dedication. No matter your goal—losing weight, growing your business, quitting smoking, decluttering your home, or making any meaningful life change—real transformation must begin with honest reflection. One of the most powerful lines in the book says it best: *"An enormous difference exists between deciding . . . and doing."* That space, that quiet interstice between intention and action, is where real change breathes. It's the moment we know what no longer serves us, and we go for what comes next. This book doesn't just acknowledge that gap; it gives readers the tools and clarity to cross it. And in doing so, it reminds us that meaningful change is not accidental—it is chosen, practiced, and lived. Well done, my dear friend!"

— Lisa Geraci Rigoni, Owner & Chief Declutter Officer of The Organizing Mentors; Author of the #1 Bestseller, *17 Spatulas and the Man Who Fried an Egg*

"I picked up this book hoping to better understand how to manage my life and career. A huge ask. To my elation, mission accomplished. Yet it also spoke to me on an even deeper level, helping me better understand myself and reminding me of what's *really* important: a genuine love for people, uncompromising values, a solid work ethic, and a desire to excel. Keeping focused on what's truly important in our everyday lives as well as at work, makes all the difference. This completely shifted my perspective. Now I've been more intentional, calmer, and less hard on myself when things don't go as planned. It's one of those books that stays with you for a lifetime."

—David Vigil, Partner NewWings Consulting, LLC

"I believe all but one manager I've served under in my nine-year career could have maintained and increased my loyalty had they only a shred of this book to guide them. And myself too, if only I had some understanding, I might have been sympathetic instead of frustrated. For all the blind people in sales there's a deaf manager in their rear-view mirror."

—Clay Lee, Sales Professional

"*Managing* to S.M.I.L.E. speaks directly to a challenge every leader knows well: the difference between managing people and empowering them to *self*-manage themselves. Steve Rigby offers a clear, practical model that shifts leadership away from control and toward ownership—without lowering standards. In my field of mortgage banking, our highest performers are already *self*-managed. This book shows leaders how to create more of them. If you care about sustainable production, healthy culture, and long-term leadership development, this book will sharpen how you lead."

—Bill Rogers, President & CEO
Homeowners Financial Group USA

"Steve Rigby's newest book has opened my eyes to so much I've been missing in my 60-some-odd years on earth. As his editor, I began reading the manuscript and realized, *hey, wait a minute, not only do I need to proofread this but need to grasp it—to take it to heart.* So, as I proofed his words, typing on my keyboard with arched fingers, I also drank in his advice, like a deer thirsty for mountain water. It all just made sense—and I've started applying much about *self*-managing myself to build my home business into a more robust venture. Especially leveraging how to build better long-term relationships with my clients.

But the journey doesn't end there. I also looked at many of the principles Steve weaves through his pages to empower me in my personal life. Like how to find an accountability partner in a way that really works and leads to refreshing changes. So illuminating. Thankfully, I'm navigating life now feeling more energetic and inspired about my personal and professional life. Steve, I just want to say, 'Thank you, sir, for your timely wisdom, humor, and guidance. It's never too late, or I guess too early, to start learning how to become *self*-managed.' The thirst of this 'parched deer' has been quenched through *Managing* to S.M.I.L.E., and I give it two thumbs up, plus eight more digits, all lifted off my keyboard in a 10-finger salute."

— Karen Steinmann, Freelance Editor
Expert Editing, Vibrant Writing

"*Managing* to S.M.I.L.E. offers a compelling guide demonstrating that excellence isn't reserved for a select few—it's accessible to anyone committed to cultivating purposeful habits and adopting a service-first mentality. This book deserves a place alongside classics like *The Go-Giver* and *A Journey into the Heroic Environment* in any reader's collection of transformative leadership literature."

—Rodney Hall, President of Rodney Hall Executive Search

"Having the privilege of knowing both the author and the heart behind the main character, this story—and how it changed me in such positive ways—is especially meaningful to me. What I love most about *Managing* to S.M.I.L.E. is how effortlessly it connects good intentions with real action. Through relatable stories and moments that feel familiar, the messages come to life in ways that honestly encourage me. This book doesn't just teach; it gently inspires you to show up, take ownership, and grow. I absolutely love it!"

—Jen Slater, Director of Sales
Gracepoint Homes

"When Steve first approached me with reading the manuscript to *Managing* to S.M.I.L.E.—How One *Manages* to Create a Culture of *Self*-Management, I have to admit, I was a little suspicious of the concept of *self*-management. With my decades of experience, a leader's role in accountability and coaching has been essential to wildly successful salespeople. But, I was looking at the book from the wrong perspective. After reading it, I realize it's not about the manager. It's about the person—one's personal accountability to own their success.

My paradigm has shifted, and now I can't stress this enough: the ones that *own* their success actively seek advice, mentorship, and accountability. While this book benefits managers, it really speaks to the person seeking excellence.

Steve, this is your best work yet! I look forward to sharing this with every team member in our organization. It will be a difference maker, no matter the position. This applies to *all* of us! Thank you for your unique perspective. It will be an epiphany to everyone who takes the time to absorb and apply its content!"

—Michael Fraley, Division President
Oakwood Homes

Managing to . . .

S.m.i.l.e.

How One *Manages* to Create a Culture of *Self*-Management

Steve M. Rigby

Library of Congress Cataloging-in-Publication Data

Rigby, Steve Michael

Managing to S.M.I.L.E.: How One *Manages* to Create a Culture of *Self*-Management

1. Title

Hardcover ISBN: 979-8-218-90094-6
Paperback ISBN: 979-8-218-91499-8

Editor: Karen Steinman
Rear Cover Photo: Rita Ramirez

For Susan, my wife, my soul mate.
You are my greatest blessing.

Contents

Foreword

Sometimes you never know where life will take you. One minute you're talking to a mentor as a sounding board, and the next you're asked to be the lead character in his new book and to also write the Foreword! When the universe speaks . . . a.k.a. Steve Rigby—a homebuilding icon who served as the national trainer for three of the nation's top-ten builders before founding his consulting firm—you listen! When he approached me with an idea that could turn around struggling management and sales teams, forever change the culture of how the corporate world manages their employees, and help individuals learn to become *self*-managed—to hold *themselves* accountable—I answered with a resounding yes! Anytime I can give back, and help people grow, organizations thrive, teams flourish, and everyone at every level achieve the respect and success they deserve, I'm all in!

Fresh out of college, I enjoyed jobs in cellular sales and then pharmaceuticals. But my calling, like Steve's, was home-building. For the past quarter-century—the early years in sales, the later (and majority) in management—I've experienced it all. From hot markets to recessions, from thriving to surviving, and everything in between, change was the one constant I could always count on. But the one thing that *never* changed is what Steve Rigby taught me at the beginning of this career. I learned the importance of genuinely caring about people, and putting their needs and interests first. I have sold and managed to that philosophy of serving others ever since. It has served me well.

So, as I dove into the manuscript, I was not surprised this philosophy lies at the core of this book. And how compelling, when I also discovered it's far from just a business book—it's also a book about life. The importance of health and fitness is woven into the fabric of the storyline, as is quality of life, especially in making time for what and who is most important to us. Even help for those battling addiction . . . yes, you heard me right, addiction . . . finds a place within these pages.

Though Steve's first two books were hugely successful . . . I must brag . . . I'm convinced this one proves his best work, yet! *Managing* to S.M.I.L.E. is a game-changer, personally and professionally. It's powerful. Touching. Inspiring. Moving. I cried as I completed the last page, and that rarely happens with any book. All I could think about was all the people whose lives will be changed if they *do*—not *decide*, but *do*—what is revealed before them in black and white.

So, sit back and enjoy my fun and exciting journey as I'm introduced to keys, imaginary men, frogs, magic mirrors, history, a model, and a tricycle from the most successful and dynamic professionals in health and fitness, real estate, hospitality, and homebuilding. If you don't finish this book with a new perspective . . . if you don't feel empowered to control your life and claim your rights . . . if you're not inspired and energized . . . and if you're not wearing a big, beautiful S.M.I.L.E. that stretches from ear to ear . . . re-read it. You missed something the first time!

Soni Graves *(You'll discover my credentials soon enough, and how to properly pronounce my name.)*

Introduction

"The most powerful control we can ever attain is to be in control of ourselves."
~ Chris Page

It's odd the things you remember as a child. Writing this book about *self*-management brought me back to a black-and-white TV show I watched in the early 1950s. For those doing the math, yes, that puts me in my mid-seventies. And just so you know, I'm still a child inside. My wife, Susan, will attest to that!

Back to the show. It was *The Howdy Doody Show* and starred a puppet dressed in a cowboy outfit. His name was Howdy. Although I was only four years old, I noticed several things about Howdy. He was funny and made me laugh. I liked that. Though fully grown, he was much shorter than I. That didn't make sense. Most of all, his movements seemed awkward and jerky. I asked my mother why. "Howdy isn't real, son," she explained, gently patting my hand. "He's a puppet."

"What's a *puppet*?" I asked.

"It's a little character made out of wood."

Huh? That seemed a little strange, I said to myself. "If he's not real, how does he move?" Curiosity was one of my stronger traits as a child. Still is today.

"By strings," she answered, "attached to his body."

That, too, sounded strange. "Who's controlling them?"

"A person."

"Where's the person pulling them?" I was persistent, too.

"Above the curtains on the stage. They're out of sight."

That's not right, I thought. *Someone, even like Howdy, being controlled by someone else? Maybe that's why whomever is pulling his strings is hiding behind a curtain. They're ashamed!* As a child, I had a great deal of empathy for those less fortunate than I was—another trait I still possess to this day.

Around that same time, my parents took me to the movie theater to watch the Disney movie *Pinocchio.* And what did I see play out on the big screen? Another puppet . . . with strings . . . being controlled by someone else.

Although Howdy and Pinocchio shared a commonality, it's what they did *not* have in common that stood out to me. Howdy's friend, Buffalo Bob—the host of the show who interacted with Howdy—was okay with his friend being controlled by someone else. Yet, Geppetto—Pinocchio's creator—did *not* want his creation to remain a puppet. He dreamed that Pinocchio would one day become a *real* boy.

And therein, I suggest, lies the difference between those who *manage* their employees and those who want to *empower* them to become *self*-managed.

This book explores how those who wear the title of manager or leader can learn to cut the strings of those they oversee. To become Geppetto. To bring out the *real* person that lies within us all. Perhaps even more critical than learning *how* to accomplish this is discovering *why* it's so important.

Empowering others to become stronger and more confident, particularly in taking control of their lives and claiming their rights, is at the heart of this book. I pray that dream is at the heart of who you are as well. If it is, this book will be a Godsend—for you, and those you know and love.

Section 1:
WHEN THE STUDENT IS READY

From Laughter to Legend

Have you ever been somewhere, and out of the blue, you hear a voice—one you haven't heard for many years—and your mind is reeling? You're thinking, wait, how can that person be here, right where I am, at this time and place in my life?

Soni was having that moment. And it was no small matter. It had been a "voice of hope and inspiration" for her that had done nothing short of alter the course of her life and her career.

Determined to find that special someone, she worked her way through the outdoor dining area of the restaurant where she had just dined . . . until she spotted him.

Rolly—a stunning parrot both in beauty and stature, two feet in height. His body was a bright yellow, with wings and tail feathers a vibrant shade of blue. He was dining with a lady who appeared to be hanging onto the parrot's every word.

As Soni stood there in disbelief, her memory took her to a similar setting. There, she was captivated to learn how Rolly—the same blue and yellow, two-foot-tall parrot—became a sales trainer.

A sales trainer? A parrot? Incredibly crazy, but true.

She recalled how Rolly had lived with a top trainer for IBM and Dale Carnegie. And this trainer would practice his skills and material on Rolly. And over time, Rolly picked up everything the trainer knew—how to sell *and* how to train.

And because he could sound more human than most humans and loved interacting with people, Rolly was asked to become a trainer himself, joining the top trainer eventually. With his wit, charm, and creativity, Rolly made training fun. What other trainers could fly into a room, hang upside down from a light fixture, or ride around on a ceiling fan? Rolly was different! Special! And he impacted a lot of lives.

That all happened in Dallas, she recalled. *What is Rolly doing outside of Austin? I don't want to interrupt his dinner, but I must at least say hello. I doubt he'll remember me. It's been twenty years.*

At that moment, the parrot's dining companion stepped away. *This is my chance,* she thought. She briskly approached his table. "Rolly, is that you? I'd recognize that laughter and voice from anywhere. Is that really you?"

Perched on a barstool at a high-top table, Rolly immediately turned her direction. Recognizing his former student, he extended his wings to offer her a warm embrace. "Soni? Yes, ma'am, it's me! It's so great to see you!" he uttered in disbelief.

"You remembered me *and* my name!"

"With your glowing smile and charming personality, how could I ever forget you?"

Soni blushed.

"What a pleasant surprise to see you here. Last I recall, Houston was home."

"It still is, Rolly. My husband and our teenagers are busy this weekend with summer plans with their friends, so I accepted a last-minute invite to see a girlfriend on the lake. I'll be joining her shortly. What about you? Are you still in Dallas?"

"No, ma'am. I left the corporate world a few years after we met. I relocated here where I conduct much of my training. You might be interested to know we hold our graduation dinner for each class at this restaurant to celebrate the experience. A business associate invited me here tonight. She just stepped away for an important call. Please tell me you have a few minutes to join us."

"I'd be honored," Soni agreed, taking a seat. "You sure she won't mind?"

"She's a people-person like you. I'm certain she'd love to meet you. We just finished our meal, but can I get you anything?"

"I'm fine, thanks," Soni held up a plastic cup. "I've got a to-go iced tea from dinner."

"Excellent. So, how have you been?"

"I'm blessed, Rolly," she smiled radiantly. "Thanks to you and what I learned from your training, I became a very successful salesperson in the Houston market for a national homebuilder. What you taught me changed my life."

"I'm not at all surprised by your success." Rolly leaned in toward Soni. "I thank you for the kind words, but at best, all I did was make a contribution. What you've become was already inside you: a genuine love for people . . . uncompromising values . . . a solid work ethic . . . and a desire to excel. You took the knowledge I shared and the skills I helped you develop, and you made it happen! As the line in the '70s song goes, 'Oz never did give nothing to the Tin Man, that he didn't, didn't already have.' "

"You're so sweet, Rolly, and I love that song. You always made me feel as if I could do anything."

"That's because you could! Are you still in sales?"

"No, sir. For over a decade, I managed a sales team for another national builder. Several years ago, I became their VP of operations. Recently, I was promoted to city manager, where I run a division."

"Well done, Soni. You are amazing."

"Thank you. What's more amazing is that recently, a friend gave me a copy of **S.M.I.L.E.**[1] You should have seen my face when I learned *you* were the one who turned Sherri's real estate career around. Sherri's story—featured in **S.M.I.L.E.**, as you know—was certainly a showstopper for me. I loved the book so much, I bought copies for our team. When I told them you trained me, they were envious. In their eyes, you're a legend."

Rolly smiled. "Legend might be a little much, Soni. Still, I'm flattered. All I did was connect a talented group of people to a lady who needed to learn to **S.M.I.L.E.** *They* are the ones who deserve all the accolades."

---

[1] **S.M.I.L.E.**, the title of the Amazon bestselling book on sales, is an acronym for five essentials that Sherri learns. ***S*** says to keep it SIMPLE for her *and* her guests. ***M*** stands for ME—she is responsible for building her business from referrals. ***I*** means to IDENTIFY the INDIVIDUAL—the personalities of her guests. ***L*** prompts her to break the sale into LITTLE decisions that simplify the bigger ones. ***E*** reminds her to ENJOY everyone she meets and everything she does.

The Universe

I love your humility, Rolly. Always have. You might be interested to know I've been planning to call you. And now, out of nowhere, you appear. It's like the universe heard me." Soni reached into her handbag for her phone. "That reminds me, I need to put this back on 'Respectful Mode.' That simple courtesy you taught Sherri has been a game changer for me—personally and professionally!"

"I've been told it's helped a lot of folks. And thank you for your respect. Mine's been on it the entire evening." With an inquisitive look, Rolly touched his wing tip to his beak. "You say you were planning on calling me. Because . . . ?"

"Two reasons. First, I wanted to congratulate you on **S.M.I.L.E.** Now, I can check that off my list. Second, I'm worried about our sales managers. I'm unsure of how to help them be successful in managing their people. I'm concerned . . ."

"Soni," Rolly interjected at that moment as his dinner guest returned, "please forgive me, but I must introduce you to Ester Impastato, a friend and business associate. Ester, this is Soni Graves, one of my best students ever!" As Soni stood to greet her, Rolly continued, "She noticed me dining here and came over to say hello. I asked her to join us."

"I'm glad she did," Ester replied with a smile as they shook hands and took their seats. "I love your name, Soni. May I ask how it's spelled?"

"Sure. It's S-O-N-I. It's often mispronounced as Sony, like the record company. I tell people it's like Donnie with an 'S.' Soni. It's a pleasure to meet you, Ester."

"Thank you, Soni. That makes it easy to get it right. It's always a pleasure to meet one of Rolly's protégés. You'd be surprised how often this happens. But I must say, I don't recall him ever using the words 'one of my best students ever' when introducing them. You must be pretty special."

Soni blushed. "Rolly is the one who's special, as you likely know. If I may ask, I'm curious how the two of you met?"

"My husband, Rob, and I own a private gym in north Austin. Rolly visited us some time back in hopes of learning more about accountability from the health and fitness industry. Accountability is a key concept in the book **S.M.I.L.E.** After learning more about it, we purchased copies for our team and provided training on the concept. They loved it."

"We were just talking about it," Soni smiled. "It's only the best book on sales ever written, and I think I've read them all! Much like you, we got copies for our team and also trained them on it."

Suddenly, a puzzled look appeared on Soni's face. "Please forgive me, Ester, but I must ask . . . When I was invited to Rolly's training years ago, we were made aware that he was a parrot. When Rolly came to visit you and Rob, did you know he wasn't a . . . well . . . a *person*?"

Ester grinned, somewhat amused by Soni's question. "No, ma'am, we had only spoken by phone. After explaining his reason for calling, we arranged a meeting time at our gym. We did find it interesting that he asked if animals were allowed. We assumed he was inquiring about service animals." Ester playfully nudged Rolly's shoulder. "You know how he loves to mess with people. And let's face it, he sounds more human than most and is without question a better communicator."

"That he is," Soni agreed.

"When he flew in for our initial meeting," Ester confessed, "we were all astonished. Needless to say, he was the talk of the entire gym. Now everyone has gotten used to him, much like at this restaurant. That said, he still gets approached on occasion to pose for pictures or autograph copies of the book."

"Enough about me," Rolly interrupted. "Soni, why don't you start over with your second reason for wanting to contact me. I want Ester to hear it. I think you're about to discover the 'universe' may have interceded yet again."

A Matter of Concern

I'm beginning to feel that, too," Soni agreed as she turned to Ester. "I was explaining that I was concerned about our sales managers. Ester, neither I nor they have had any formal management training, and I'm unsure of how to help them. I fear that much of our past success has been a result of favorable market conditions. However, the market is changing. Overall, sales and profitability are decreasing."

"You should be concerned," Rolly acknowledged. "But you said *overall.* Can you please talk about that a bit more?"

"Sure. Not *all* our people are struggling. A few are doing better than ever. Then a handful are performing okay. But the majority are nowhere close to what they're capable of doing. Further, none of what we're experiencing can be attributed to product, price, amenities, location, or available homes for sale. The playing field is pretty level."

"Is there anything else you can tell us?" Rolly inquired.

"Yes, sir. Searching for answers, we mystery-shopped them. We noticed the few excelling focused on putting people first, using manners, treating shoppers like guests, connecting on a personal level, and making them feel important. They asked all the right questions and gained a deep understanding of their guests' situation. As a result, they reduced the number of homes to consider, saving everyone time and stress. In addition, through the little decisions they helped them make along the way, it was easy for their shoppers to want to say yes to buying."

"You know what you're telling us, don't you?" Ester asked.

Soni held up her hand and wiggled her fingers. "I do, Ester. They're doing what Sherri committed to Rolly that she would do—they're holding themselves acCOUNTable to applying what they learned from **S.M.I.L.E.**"

"I would agree. What about the other two groups?"

"The okay group was applying bits and pieces. As for those falling far short of expectations, hardly any."

"That's unfortunate," Rolly noted, "but not uncommon."

Houston, We Have an Opportunity

"Uncalled for might be a better way to describe it, Rolly. Our management team was *not* happy!" Soni exclaimed, shaking her head in dismay. "I just don't get it. We strive to hire the right people. Train them well. Care for them. Treat them fairly, with respect. We manage them all the same: set goals, specify activities to perform, and monitor progress. We want to think we set them up for success Yet, not all seem to appreciate that. Rolly, do you think we have a management problem?"

"We feel your frustration," Rolly nodded. "Ester, reflecting on the many talks you, Rob, and I have had on this topic, I'd appreciate your thoughts, especially considering that you and Rob are having success with your people applying what they learned from **S.M.I.L.E.** In your opinion, do you feel Soni has a management problem?"

Ester confidently stated, "Soni, based on what you shared, I respectfully suggest that what you have is a *self*-management *opportunity*."

Taken aback by her answer, Soni looked at Rolly first, then back at Ester. "Why do I feel like Sherri must have felt in **S.M.I.L.E.** when Rolly asked her to rotate the page with the curved line she had drawn, causing her to change her perspective? Ahh . . . a *self*-management *opportunity* as opposed to a management problem. Are you suggesting I need to look at managing from a different perspective?"

Ester addressed Rolly. "Now I know why you describe Soni as one of your best students ever." She turned to look eye-to-eye with Soni. "Most perceptive. Yes, ma'am, that's precisely what we're suggesting. You might benefit by looking at managing in a different way—actually in a most simple way."

"Heaven knows, I love simple. So, how do I get there?"

"Soni," Rolly responded, "I'm confident you could begin to discover the answer to your *self*-management *opportunities* when your schedule permits a visit to their gym."

"Then, how quickly can we make this happen?" Soni inquired. "The sooner, the better, as far as I'm concerned."

Rolly paused. "This has certainly caught your attention, Soni. And I appreciate the urgency of your predicament. Since you're in town, and assuming Ester and Rob can make time for you, is this weekend possible? They will likely need several hours of your time."

"For this, I'll make the time! My girlfriend is pretty easy-going, living on 'lake time' you know. I'm sure she'll understand if I slip away for a few hours." Soni turned to Ester. "I know it's short notice, but can you and Rob possibly fit me in?" she asked, almost pleading.

After checking her phone's calendar, Ester nodded yes. "Soni, for one of Rolly's *best students ever*, Rob and I will make the time. If Sunday afternoon at two works for you, we'll see you then. You can google BigTexGym.com to get directions from our website."

"That's perfect, Ester. Thank you so! That gives me all day Saturday with my girlfriend, and I can see you and Rob on my way back to Houston Sunday. I'll be early, and like Sherri, I'm always willing to learn."

"But are you also willing to travel?" Rolly inquired. "I ask because if you're serious about this, I'll begin making calls tonight in hopes of scheduling visits for you for next week with some more talented, giving people. They'll teach you how to apply what Ester and Rob will share, helping you help your sales managers and their salespeople to become *self*-managed. Call me after Sunday's visit with Ester and Rob to discuss details."

"Yes, sir, Rolly, I'm dead serious. Holly James, my boss, is a huge believer in educating and helping her teams grow and succeed. She says, 'We make time for what's important!'

Considering the market conditions, I'm confident she and I will make this work." Soni held up her hands and wiggled her fingers. "I also promise I'll be committed to holding myself acCOUNTable, just like Sherri."

"We would expect nothing less," Rolly exclaimed. "When speaking with Holly, you might mention that what you will learn goes far beyond sales. It's applicable to *all* managers and their people in *all* departments. From top to bottom, the entire organization can benefit."

"I didn't want to get ahead of myself, but I was already thinking about that. Which makes it all the more imperative that she and I make this happen. And I assure you, we will!"

"I have no doubt, Soni. Now, if you ladies will excuse me, *I* need to make something happen. I need to take care of the tab."

Ester smiled as she waved a paid receipt. "Sir, it's already taken care of. Why don't you give us a big hug, and we will all call it an evening?"

"I can't believe you picked up our meal again!"

"And I can't believe you fell for the old 'I've got an important call to make' ploy. Pretty lame if you ask me!"

Everyone laughed, hugged, and said their goodbyes.

Section 2:
THE KEYS TO *SELF*-MANAGEMENT

An Uplifting Environment

Soni, please forgive me," Ester apologized. "I wasn't able to properly greet you when you came in. As you witnessed, I was busy helping the sweetest couple and their ten-year-old son—who all just committed to join as a family!"

"No need to apologize," Soni said, giving Ester a warm hug. "I did arrive early and wouldn't have expected you to be free. I must say, based on what I just saw as I took a quick tour of your gym, I'd jump at the opportunity to join here, too."

"Thank you, Soni. We believe we have something for everyone, regardless of their fitness level or experience. From bodybuilding, to strongman, to powerlifting, and everything in between, we feel we have the services and expertise to help people reach their goals."

"I believe you. While getting your address on your website, I noticed in addition to your many accolades, you were voted 'Gym of the Month' by Bodybuilding.com and 'Top 10 Gym in the World' by SpotMeBro.com while racking up twenty-eight million YouTube views! Impressive!"

"Thank you, again. Rob and I are grateful we get to do something we feel makes a difference. And a special thanks for the difference it made chatting in the parking lot Friday evening after Rolly left. I left convinced that you are one . . . cool . . . lady!"

"Likewise, Ester. And thank you. Todd, my husband, tells me that all the time," Soni confided with a wink. "Of course, I think it's only because he knows what's good for him."

Ester smiled as well. "It's no surprise that your Todd and my Rob have a lot in common. Speak of the devil, I see he's coming to join us." She gave her husband a peck on the cheek and introduced him to their guest for the afternoon.

"Soni, I would like you to meet Rob, my better half. Rob, this is Soni Graves, the lady I told you about that Rolly introduced me to at dinner."

Soni stared in disbelief as a mountain of a man stood before her. She knew he was big from the pictures on their website but had no idea he was that massive. She gingerly extended her hand to shake his. "Rob, it's a genuine pleasure to meet you. Please promise you won't crush my hand."

Rob gently held Soni's fingertips as he politely kissed the back of her hand and bowed. "My dear, I would never harm one of God's beautiful creations."

Soni turned a dozen shades of red. "Oh my, is he always this charming, Ester?"

"He is a gentleman in every sense of the word. He is also full of it," Ester joked as she gave Rob a playful slap on his wrist. "Which is why I, and everyone here, love him so."

"What a compliment for *your* own strongman, Ester."

Still smiling and a bit flushed, Soni turned to address Rob. "Forgive me, but I must ask how you've managed to get in such incredible shape."

Humbled, Rob softly replied, "I'd be happy to share that, Soni. But first, allow me to offer you what we offered Rolly during his first visit. Let's move away from the front desk to a quieter area where we can sit and talk without interruptions. May we also offer you some refreshments?"

"Thank you, but I'm fine for now. I just finished an iced tea." Rob's comment regarding interruptions reminded her to put her phone on 'Respectful Mode' before she put it away.

The Stage Is Set

The three took a seat around a small, round table on a stage overlooking a substantial portion of the gym. "This is an amazing vantage point. You can see almost everything and everyone from here," Soni remarked.

"Rolly made the same observation," Ester revealed. "And since it was his first time to visit a gym, he asked if he could take pictures. He also requested we tell him a bit about some of our members and what they were doing in the different areas."

"Would you mind doing the same for me?" Soni asked. "I'm interested in what you might have shared."

"Gladly. Let's begin with the members over by the windows. They are benefiting from a cardiovascular workout. The gentleman in the gray T-shirt and plaid shorts is a minister. He's here to drop a few pounds. Next month, he's officiating his daughter's wedding and wants to fit into his favorite suit."

"What a special moment for him to treasure. Is weight loss a common goal for many members?"

"It is, Soni. Nationally, one-third of all gym members go there to lose weight.[2] Our trainer Michael is helping him. When Michael isn't holding boot camp or kids' fitness classes, he specializes in weight loss transformation, including customized diet and meal planning. That's important to offer, as the latest Mayo Clinic report revealed that less than three percent of Americans live a healthy lifestyle.[3] Michael told us this gentleman has dropped twenty pounds in just thirteen weeks—right on target!"

"Good for him!" Soni exclaimed. "I love that you conduct classes for kids, too."

"We try to offer help to any person, for any reason, at any age," Rob shared. "Over on the treadmills, the couple wearing camouflage sweats are Air Force recruiters. They're training to run their third marathon this year."

"That's quite an accomplishment. I learned from your website that both of you were in the military. Thank you for your service. My stepfather served in the Army."

"On behalf of Ester and me, we thank you. And please express our gratitude to your stepfather. We proudly offer discounts to military personnel, police officers, and fire-fighters. They are special to us, as is the silver-haired gentleman on the exercise bike next to them. He recently sold his business and now devotes his spare time to volunteer work with local charities."

"I admire people who give back."

"As do we. He is here to stay fit by strengthening his heart muscles and improving lung capacity."

---

[2] Statista, 2021

[3] https://www.thenationshealth.org/content/46/5/16.2

"He just celebrated his seventy-fifth birthday with us," Ester added. "We lit candles on energy bars, and the entire gym sang happy birthday. It was a special moment!"

"Seventy-five!" Soni exclaimed in total surprise. "I would have guessed he was in his late fifties, at best."

"Everyone does. Researchers have found that, biologically speaking, individuals who engage in high levels of physical activity are, on average, nine years younger than those who are sedentary.[4] When anyone asks him why he's here, he'll boldly say, 'I'm not letting the *old man* in!' "

"I love his attitude! If I'm not mistaken, that's a Toby Keith song from Clint Eastwood's movie *The Mule*."

"It is, Soni. You know your songs and your movies."

"And you know your people."

"It's all about our people. They are family. It's the reason we're here. Again, we help them get where they want to be."

"I like the way you put that," Soni asserted. "You know, instead of us 'managing' our people to get them where *we* want them to be, we would be better off 'helping' them get where *they* want to be."

"It would appear you're already looking at managing from a different perspective," Ester affirmed. "The lady who just waved at us certainly knows where she wants to be, personally and professionally. She's a top Realtor in Austin. Her workouts help her deal with stress and tone her body. She recently gave birth to twin girls and is working to regain her figure."

---

[4] Franciscan Health www.franciscanhealth.org>community>blog / https://universe.byu.edu/2017/06/28/byu-research-suggests-exercise-reverses-cellular-aging-process1

"Are you sure she's not here to just get a break, on both accounts? A challenging career *and* twins. I'm impressed!"

"Us, too. Moving over to the area with the weight equipment, the gentleman in the black shorts and tank top is a local rancher. He is an accomplished powerlifter."

"Next to him," Rob interjected, "the couple using the dumbbells are prepping for a bodybuilding competition. They own a chain of restaurants—quite the dynamic pair. Coaching them are Steven and Mikaela. They're both trainers with us and professional bodybuilders, too. In a bit, they'll all be up here on stage using the mirrors behind us to work on their posing techniques. Learning to pose is a critical component in preparing for competition."

"Now I know why you have this stage. For posing."

Unlocking the Doors

Ester responded with a twinkle in her eye, "Believe it or not, Rolly chose to do some posing on this very stage."

"Rolly? Posing?" Soni quipped, "That must have been entertaining! I hope you got pictures."

"Actually, it was a series of questions he posed to us based on research he'd done on gyms," Ester smiled broadly. "First, he asked if we would be interested in learning about what he proposed are five things that everyone who gets a gym membership likely has in common."

Rob spoke, "Before we could respond, he made it even more enticing. He was confident there is a sixth thing that will determine whether the first five work."

"This sounds intriguing. I need to write these down," Soni remarked as she reached for her handbag under her seat.

"You could do that, or . . . "

Ester teasingly interrupted, "Or . . . you could use this." She handed Soni a custom portfolio from her lap.

"After Rolly's visit, he texted Ester and me the most creative images that made what we are about to share so easy to visualize and understand. They have become part of his ***Self*-Management Program**, which he is about to roll out. You will find them in this little gift from the three of us."

"*Little* gift?" Soni excitedly examined it. "Carrying handle, three-ring binder with blank tabs, a removable clipboard, an organizer for iPad or tablet and phone, then pens, *your* business cards, and black faux leather that just happens to match my handbag. Oh, my!" She reached out to squeeze Ester's hand. "Somebody put a little time and thought into this. Thank you all so very, VERY much!"

"You were so 'together' when we met the other night. I thought this would give you a way to keep everything together that we will give you, as well as what you will receive from others whom we expect you to meet this week."

"Fortunately," Rob mentioned, "a business nearby specializes in items like this. We couldn't resist."

"I'm thankful you didn't!"

Soni reflected on Rob and Ester's earlier comments. "Rob, you say Rolly initially texted you the images from his phone of what's in here. And Ester just mentioned he took pictures with it during that first visit. I'm curious if the two of you were impressed by the special harness he had under his wings, where he kept his phone?"

"Were we ever!" Rob admitted. "You realize 'concealed carry' is legal in Texas, so we weren't sure what he was about to pull out from under his wing." Everyone chuckled.

"Soni," Rob grinned, "we're just so happy to share all this with you. The commonalities between everyone getting a gym membership involves five questions. We'll now briefly touch on each one. Afterward, we can discuss them in more detail. You will discover the images behind the first blank tab."

Soni turned the tab to reveal the first image.

"How creative!" she asserted in admiration. "I love the visual. I see the question clearly posed. I assume there's a reason for the image of the Key, as well as for the word **What** emphasized?"

"There is. **What**, printed larger than the other words, indicates its importance in the question itself. You'll see that occur in the remaining questions as well."

"Rob, dear, you might recall that Rolly teased us due to the 'extra-special' reason he would later reveal for those words printed prominently on each Key."

"You're right. Thanks for the reminder. As for the image of the Key, it's to symbolize that each question is *key* to unlocking the doors that will lead our members to being able to *self*-manage their health and fitness needs."

"Why do I get the feeling," Soni speculated, "that these Keys, and the doors they open, might apply to more than just health and fitness?"

"You never know," Ester declared with a smile.

Soni smiled back. "I am so excited! Please continue."

Rob obliged. "First, he asked if we felt each member had given thought to **What** their current situation is now: too thin, too heavy, fatigued, weak or frail, out of shape, lack of stamina, not happy with the way their body looks, etc.?"

"We agreed," Ester confessed. "That is where everything begins. Before we know where we want to be, we have to be honest with ourselves regarding what our situation is now."

"That's the same as the HAVE NOW question Bob taught Sherri in the ***S*** in **S.M.I.L.E.**," Soni explained. "What her guests were LOOKING FOR lacked reason without the awareness of what they HAVE NOW."

"Precisely!" Ester agreed. "If their current situation pertains to the way they see themselves, we encourage them to take 'before' pictures. Being able to refer to them can be motivating as they see progress being made."

"Plus," Rob added, "many see value in also writing down where they are starting from: weight, body measurements, percent of body fat, blood pressure, or resting heart rate. Soni, if you turn to the next page, you will discover Rolly's continuation of Bob's HAVE NOW question that sets the stage for what they are LOOKING FOR."

As Soni turned the page, Ester spoke up, "When Rolly asked if our members had likely thought about **Where** they wanted to be—their ideal weight, overall fitness, percentage of body fat, increased strength, bodybuilder physique, toned look —we responded with a resounding yes!"

"And if they don't have a clear vision in their mind," Rob offered, "we help them picture that 'end in mind' with questions. We have learned that if we ask the right questions and listen closely, we and they will gain a much clearer understanding of **Where** they want to be."

"Ester," Soni interrupted, "this validates your statement from earlier. I believe your words were, 'We have the services and expertise to help folks reach their goals.' "

"You're a great listener!" Ester praised. "Of course, we have them write down their goals so they and we can refer to them if and when needed."

"When it comes to the Third Key and the door it opens," Rob stated, "Rolly gave us credit for already answering this one: if they knew *why* they wanted to look, or feel, or be able to perform a certain way? Flip to the next page, Soni, for this key question."

As Soni did so, she acknowledged, "You two certainly confirmed this one when you went around the room and shared with me the reason each person was here."

"Thank you, Soni," Ester said. "Their **Why** gives them the reason to get where they want to be. It motivates them to decide to get a membership, schedule their workouts, get out of bed, put on workout clothes, arrive on time, use the equipment, lift the weights, push their bodies, complete the reps, and modify their diet. Their **Why** is critical."

Soni nodded. "Yes, ma'am, it is."

"We agreed with Rolly on the first three," Rob confessed. "So, on to the Fourth Key and the door it opens."

As Soni turned the page, Ester jumped in. "Here, Rolly asked if we thought they had considered **When** they wanted this to happen—a deadline to get where they wanted to be."

"Ester, I recall you responded with a quote from Robert Herjavec that we have used for years. 'A goal without a deadline is just a dream.' "

"His quote is so applicable," Soni admitted. "Setting an expectation as to **When** they want this to happen creates urgency. It helps the dream become a reality in due time."

"So true," Rob agreed. "At this point, Rolly asked if *how* they expected to get there was likely a consideration. That key question is on the next page if you will turn to it."

"Absolutely," Soni said, turning the page.

"We felt the same. The **How** Key is another they all should have in common. Behind that door is where a plan is formulated that brings the first four together."

"That plan often begins with the number of visits to the gym each week," Ester revealed. "The amount of time allocated for each visit would typically follow, including what time of day. The activities performed, machines used, the weights lifted, number of reps, changes in diet, and required hours of sleep—they would all likely be part of that plan."

"It's **How** they get **Where** they want to be," Soni concluded. "And I would imagine this planning might require more time than all the previous questions combined."

"Almost always," Ester agreed. "But it's well worth that investment of time."

Take a Hike

At that moment, Soni's face grew puzzled as she began flipping back through the pages displaying the other Four Keys. "Hmmm . . . don't these Five Keys, and the doors they open, cover it all?"

"How do you mean?" Ester's eyes twinkled again.

"Let's equate what we just addressed to a daylong hike through one of our national parks," Soni held up her left hand and extended her index finger. "Every journey begins with finding our location on the map, which equates to **What** our current situation is now—our starting point, if you will."

"Makes sense."

Soni held up her second finger. "Next, we determine **Where** we want to be . . . our destination . . . **Where** we are headed on our hike. We might even circle it on the map."

Ester nodded in agreement.

Adding her third finger, Soni continued, "With the Third Key, we know **Why** we want to be there . . . our motivation . . . the payoff of what's waiting for us."

"Completely agree, Soni."

Offering her fourth finger, she added, "Next, we have determined **When** we want to get there, including our return time in this case. Now we can establish a timeline of when to start, as well as the pace to set."

"We're with you so far," Ester agreed. Rob also nodded.

Soni extended her thumb. "Finally, we make a plan on **How** to get there. It might begin with determining the type of hiking gear and attire we'll need, including water, food, sunscreen, and a first aid kit. We'll also decide on the trails to take and how we'll navigate them on our hike. Lastly, we'll highlight the route on our map."

"All of that we'd likely do, Soni. Very good."

"So, what is left? Why a Sixth Key? What's missing?"

"It's not *what* is left, or *what* is missing," Ester explained. "It's *who* is left. It's *who* is missing."

"Who?" Soni then added more emphasis. "*Who?* I'm confused."

"Not to worry," Ester advised. "Just remember that Rolly felt we would agree on the first five things everyone who gets a gym membership likely has in common. And Rob and I did. You recognize those are the Five Keys that unlock the five doors we just shared. But Rolly mentioned a sixth thing: *the* thing he felt would determine whether the first five actually work or not. Remember?"

"I do. Yeeeesss. And thanks for reminding me."

Decide or Do

Rob spoke up, "Before you turn to that sixth thing—the final Key—allow us to offer a scenario that Rolly presented to us at this point. I think it will help you understand its importance. You ready?"

"I was born ready!" Soni teased. "And I'm switching from confused . . . to curious."

"A great switch. Interestingly enough, we can tie Rolly's scenario to your hike. Let's say that on your hike, you come across three frogs resting on a log. At that moment, perhaps startled by you, one of the three decides to jump off. How many frogs remain on the log?"

Soni pondered, "I'm tempted to respond two. Three, minus the one who decides to jump off, equals two. Right? But knowing Rolly, there's a lesson here. So, I'm guessing three. Why? Because the one only *decided* to jump off. Did I get it?"

"You got it, Soni. There's three. The lesson? An enormous difference exists between *deciding* . . . and *doing*!"

Ester added, "Rolly helped us recognize that the first Five Keys, which unlock and open the first five doors, get our members to a point of deciding. *Deciding* to lose weight. *Deciding* to get in better shape. *Deciding* to start working out. *Deciding* to compete. *Deciding* to get a membership. In your example, *deciding* to take a hike. Or, with the frog, *deciding* to jump."

Rob spoke up, "You might recall when discussing the **Why** at the Third Key, Ester stated that it motivates our members to *decide* to get a membership, as well as *decide* to schedule the things that need to be done."

"Now I realize that until we *do* begin working out, until we *do* begin hiking, until we *do* jump, nothing changes."

"That's paramount, Soni. Until we *do*, nothing is *done*."

Six Honest Serving Men

I like the simplicity and truth in that. So, please help me with how **Who** comes into play."

"Gladly," Ester answered. "Rolly introduced us to what he called the sixth of 'Six Honest Serving Men'—a man named **Who**. A man whose name will appear on our final Key."

Soni slowly repeated the words. "Six . . . Honest . . . Serving . . . Men." With a look of astonishment, she exclaimed, "Wait a minute. Rolly has already introduced us to the first Five Serving Men, hasn't he? And their names prominently appear on each of the Five Keys: **What, Where, Why, When,** and **How.** I knew I recognized them from earlier. I could not place them until now. They are from a poem Rolly shared during his training. And it's so powerful!"

"It is, Soni. The poem was written in 1902 by English novelist, poet, and journalist Rudyard Kipling," Rob said.

Ester explained, "It's titled 'I Keep Six Honest Serving Men.' You'll find it on the next page in your portfolio."

Soni turned to the page titled I KEEP SIX HONEST SERVING MEN and read the poem aloud.

I keep six honest serving men
(They taught me all I knew);
Their names are What and Why and When
And How and Where and Who.

"In Rolly's sales training, the poem heightened our awareness of the importance of asking questions based on their names," Soni shared, "and those questions made us better listeners, which allowed us to become better influencers. The result? We could more easily help our guests move from *deciding* . . . to *doing*."

"Same here," Ester added. "For *our* purpose, they serve as Doormen who hold the Keys with the questions bearing their names. These Keys not only unlock the doors that help people *decide* to improve their health and fitness by joining our gym, but also cause them to actually show up and use it—to *do*!"

The Key to Doing

Soni," Rob commented, "if you turn to the next page, you will find the final Key—the Key to accountability."

Doing so, Soni noted, "This image is much larger than the others. That's on purpose?"

"It is. The first five—the smaller ones—are the Keys to deciding. Though important, they take a backseat to this Key. To reiterate, this larger Key of **Who** is the Key to *doing*. And this larger Key opens a larger lock, to a set of double doors."

"Okay, this is becoming more and more interesting, Rob. This prompts a number of questions. My first pertains to the second part of the question posed by the Key itself: Who is the **Who** that will ensure something *is* done, that will *hold* us accountable? Is it a manager? Is it a coworker? A trainer? A friend? A spouse? A family member? . . . Who is it?"

"Soni, it can be *any* . . . it can be *all* . . . or it can be *none* of the choices you offered," Rob playfully shared.

Know Thyself

Ester noticed Soni appeared perplexed. Sporting the slightest of grins, she said, "I warned you he was full of it. Please allow me to come to the rescue with a question for you. In your opinion, Soni, who stands the most to gain by you being held accountable?"

"Clearly, it would be me. The one option I did *not* offer. But I am thinking now that I should have."

"It *is* you. And who knows you better than anyone?"

"That, too, would be me."

"I would hope so. The fact is, you know everything about yourself. You know what you are capable of doing—your strengths. Plus, you know your limitations—what you are *not* capable of doing. Are you with me so far, Soni?"

"I am, Ester. Please continue."

"Let's begin with what we *are* capable of doing. A few individuals either know or have learned how to manage themselves. They are *self*-managed. They know what needs to be done, and they do it! My Rob is like that. Come to think of it, now might be the opportune time for him to respond to your question regarding how he managed to get in such incredible shape."

"Soni," Rob began, "I am a pretty simple guy. And as simply as I can put it, I got in this shape, and I stay in this shape, because I am *self*-managed. I have always been *self*-managed. The person I see in the mirror each day—the person I look in the eye who is staring right back at me—has always held me accountable. And I am not about to let him down!"

Ester interrupted, "Soni, the other night, Rolly described you as being *self*-managed. When I stepped away to pay the tab, I was near enough to overhear his comment that what you had become was already inside you. That you made it happen!"

"I remember his words."

"Let's not forget that Sherri is also *self*-managed. That evening, you mentioned that she promised Rolly she would hold herself accountable for what she was learning, and she did. She even made an 'Accountability List' for each day to ensure that happened."

"Same goes for *all* the people you read about in **S.M.I.L.E.**," Rob insisted. "Rolly told us that Bob, Sarah, James, John, Susan, Christophe, Ariff, and Bert were all *self*-managed."

"You can see," Ester reasoned, "that you are in good company. I told you earlier that you're one cool lady. In my book, *self*-managed people are the *coolest* of cool!"

Rob reached over to squeeze Ester's hand. "Soni, you can also add Ester to that 'cool' list. She, too, is *self*-managed. Ester's role in our business is every bit as important as mine. She, too, does what needs to be done."

Different Strokes

"Welcome to the *cool* side, Ester," Soni declared as they high-fived. "Rob shared that he sees his reflection in the mirror that holds him accountable. When I reflect on it, I hear an inner voice that speaks to me. It tells me what to do, as well as what not to do. Ester, what works for you?"

"Thank you, ma'am, for asking. I view it as a sense of conscience, a feeling that comes over me. After Rolly introduced us to **Who**, I looked up the definition of conscience and saved a screenshot on my iPad. Check this out . . ."

Soni read it aloud. *"Conscience: an inner feeling or voice viewed as acting as a guide to the rightness or wrongness of one's behavior."*

"Notice anything?" Ester quizzed.

"Yes, ma'am. It covered us both—an inner feeling or a voice that guides us."

"More searching provided more clarity." As she scrolled to the next image, Ester read, *"The inner sense of what is right or wrong in one's conduct or motives, impelling one toward right action."*

"That one registered big time with Rolly, Ester, and me!" Rob exclaimed. "It brought *action* into play. So, whether it's a stare from our reflection in the mirror . . . a voice . . . a feeling . . . or an inner sense, I believe we all would agree that it's the *action*, the *jumping*, the *doing* that matters!"

Help, I Need Somebody

"Without question," Soni emphatically agreed. "So, I must ask. For those like us who *do* hold ourselves accountable, who *are self*-managed, who *always* jump, who *always* do . . . what is the purpose of **Who**? How is our Sixth Serving Man actually *being* of service?"

"First, Rolly reminded us that **Who** is not responsible for holding us accountable. He is just holding the Key that demands we give thought to **who** actually *will* do so."

"But unlike the other Serving Men that only address one question," Ester advised, "**Who** does double duty. Along with getting the answer to **who** will *hold* us accountable, he also addresses **who** will help us."

"*Hold* . . . and now . . . *help*?" Soni asked as she contemplated Ester's answer. "Can you help me with this?"

"Sure. Let's begin with a question about control. Would you agree that *self*-managed individuals enjoy being in control of their lives?"

"Enjoy?" Soni rolled her eyes with a twinge of sarcasm in her tone. "Enjoy is an understatement. I thirst for it like it's iced tea!"

"A great comparison!" Ester laughed. "Rob and I feel the same, and we would imagine most *self*-managed people would also. Yet, being 'in control' doesn't mean we have to do it all ourselves. In fact, at times, becoming *self*-managed requires us to 'share' control with others."

"*Share* control . . . as opposed to *giving up* control? Is that what I'm hearing?"

"It is," Rob confirmed. "Let's begin with the word 'help' in the **Who** Key. Being *self*-managed does not mean we will never need help from others. Just because someone has the will, discipline, drive, determination, resolve, or grit—whatever you choose to call it—to do what needs to be done, does not mean they do it, or have done it, alone. A big part of being *self*-managed is recognizing and accepting what we do *not* know."

"Hmmm . . . That takes real courage," Soni confided.

"And humility. When we recognize what we do not know about how to do something, we should remember the importance of knowing our limitations. As Ester just discussed, *self*-managed people immediately seek out those who *do* have that knowledge and experience and ask them for help."

"I think I understand what you're saying, but can you give me an example or two?"

"Sure. Take me. Before I joined my first gym, I knew *what* my current situation was, *where* I wanted to be, *why* I wanted to be there, and *when* I wanted it to happen. But what I lacked was the knowledge of *how* to make it happen. So, I sought out those *who* had that knowledge and experience and asked them for help. Apparently, it worked."

"Did it ever!" Soni admitted, rolling her eyes again.

Rob blushed this time. "Thank you again, Soni. It was the same with my military career. I was determined to become a superior soldier. However, I was unsure what that entailed. So, I welcomed help from my superiors who did know. They taught me the *how*."

"Help can also come from books," Ester said. "What Rob and I didn't know about running a business, we learned from business books. Help can come in many forms."

"I get it now," Soni admitted. "The other night, Rolly mentioned the knowledge and skills he helped me begin to develop from his training. He helped me with what to do and how to do it. During my entire career as well as in my new role, I've received help from my managers and coworkers with a myriad of things I've needed to learn."

"Same as with the help Sherri received," Rob proclaimed. "We've all had to *share* control to *secure* control eventually."

A Paradox of Sorts

"S*hare* to *secure*," Soni repeated. "An interesting paradox for the first part of this Key: **Who** will help? . . . Can it also apply to the second part?"

"Yes, ma'am. If our answer to the second part of the question is that we are *not* capable of holding ourselves accountable, then we need to seek out the person—or people—we'll share that control with, who *will* hold us accountable."

"So, a clear distinction exists between someone who will *help* us and someone who will *hold* us accountable, correct?" Soni looked at Rob.

"Only with what they are tasked with doing. *Help* is about *a*-bility—about providing knowledge or aid in developing a skill. *Hold* is about *account*-ability—making certain we show up and *do* what must be done."

"*A*-bility versus *account*-ability. I like that," Soni confided. "I must ask. Are these two different people, or can one person assume both roles? Plus, if needed, can we have more people involved with either or both?"

"Fair questions," Ester answered. "Let's examine our members from earlier to see what we can learn from their experiences. Michael is *helping* our minister with the proper use of the equipment, as well as educating him on diet and meal planning—all things he doesn't know how to do on his own. At the same time, Michael is also *holding* him accountable for showing up for his scheduled consultations and workouts, including eating right and dropping the weight."

"So, Michael is performing both roles: *help* and *hold*."

"Correct. As for our recruiters, who've successfully trained for two marathons, no help is needed with all the prep and planning involved. Yet, as you might imagine, training for a marathon can become a grind. So, as a couple, they're *holding* each other accountable for showing up and sticking to it."

"I can see that. So, they're just *holding*."

"Correct again. Now, to our bodybuilding couple. One look at their physiques will tell you they have proven their commitment to doing. But posing? That's new for them. Which is why they have asked for, and are receiving, *help* from Steven and Mikaela."

"So, they're only receiving help."

"You got it. That is all they need. Did that answer your question, Soni?"

"Absolutely. We can have as few or as many people as needed *helping* or *holding*, interacting with us from two vastly different perspectives: *a*-bility versus *account*-ability."

Magic Mirror on the Wall

"Your reference to 'different perspectives' provides the perfect segway into another point about the final Key," Rob offered.

"Does it have anything to do with the double doors?"

"It does. What we're about to discover behind these doors was influenced by a fairy tale Rolly read to his little ones when they were young. It involved a mirror. Care to guess what fairy tale it might be?"

"*Snow White*?" Soni excitedly volunteered. "It was my favorite as a child. Her evil queen stepmother used a magic mirror to determine who was the fairest of them all. And that person would magically appear in the mirror."

"That's the one. Rolly suggested that as we proceed through the double doors—which **Who** has unlocked and opened for us—we should picture a long hallway. And the walls on either side are lined with magic mirrors. Can you picture this?"

"Vividly!" Soni responded.

"Above the mirrors on each wall, a question is inscribed that reminds us of the two-part question on **Who**'s Key. The question on the left wall addresses the first part. It reads . . .

MAGIC MIRRORS ON THIS WALL,

WHO WILL *HELP* ME MOST OF ALL?

Soni interrupted, "Since the second part of the Key deals with accountability, I am guessing the question on the opposite wall reads . . .

MAGIC MIRRORS ON THIS WALL,

WHO WILL *HOLD* ME ACCOUNTABLE?

Is that it?"

Rob nodded in agreement. "It is. So, back to the left wall. Rolly informed us that if we need help, we will see the face, or faces, appearing in these mirrors of those who have either offered their help or have accepted our request for their help. One face per mirror, for as many as are needed. And if we do not need help, the mirrors will be blank. You with me?"

"Yes, sir. And on the right?"

"If we *are* capable of holding ourselves accountable, when we look at those mirrors, we will only see our reflection in the first magic mirror. The others are blank."

"Makes sense. We are capable of doing it ourselves."

"You got it. But if we are *not* capable, we will not see our image. Instead, we will see the image, or images, of those who have either offered to hold us accountable or have accepted our request to do so. And once again, one face per mirror, for as many as are needed."

"Just to clarify, the way someone can appear in our mirrors is either *they* offer, and *we* accept; or *we* request, and *they* accept. Both require a mutual agreement. Is that correct?"

"Yes, ma'am, it is, Soni. It's the *only* way! Just remember that even though we are *sharing* control, we are *in* control of who is in those mirrors. We are *self*-managing ourselves."

"So, if a manager wants to help their people become *self*-managed, do they simply need to ask for permission to be in their mirrors and gain agreement to do so?"

No Strings Attached

Essentially, yes," Ester answered. "However, there are strings attached—strings the managers must be willing to let go of!"

Soni appeared confused. "Strings? What strings? Did I miss something?"

"The strings they have been pulling," Ester shared.

"You mean like strings on a puppet?" Soni guessed.

"Precisely. Rolly helped us understand that when Rob and I were managing our staff 'in the manner in which most managers manage'—his words—that we were treating them like puppets on a string. Even though we cared about them and treated them fairly and with respect, we were nothing more than puppet masters controlling their every move."

At first, Soni was shocked. "That's a rather harsh way of looking at management," she confessed. "But now I see you've painted a really good picture—Rolly has a way of doing that. Though I would like to think we mean well, that pretty much represents where we are and what we do as managers. We are above them . . . in a position of power and authority . . . pulling their strings . . . controlling their every action."

"Even with the best of intentions, Rob and I were dictating the **What, Where, Why, When, How,** and **Who**."

"The other night, I was concerned we might be *mismanaging* our team. Now I realize it's possible that they feel we are *manipulating* them. And that is the last thing we want."

"As people, we are either *self*-managed . . . or we are *being* managed. We are either *in* control . . . or *being* controlled. We are either our *own person* . . . or someone's *puppet*."

"Ester, as I look back to your answer the other evening that I actually have a *self*-management opportunity, I had no idea how profound that statement would prove to be. I have a huge *self*-management opportunity to cut the strings—to right some wrongs. And what an opportunity it is!"

The Magic of the Mirrors

Rob and I felt the same way, Soni. As someone begins taking advantage of this opportunity, what would expectations be long-term pertaining to the images of those appearing in the mirrors on either wall?"

"Is it safe to say we would expect them to disappear eventually, meaning they have fulfilled their purpose?"

"Yes, ma'am. The end goal is to only see *our* image in the first mirror on the wall on the right—the *Account*-ability wall."

"And can I assume that if instead of seeing our *image*, we can prefer . . . to hear a *voice* . . . get a *feeling* . . . or have an *inner sense*?"

"Absolutely," Ester agreed. "It's *our* magic mirror. We can have it do whatever we would like."

"I guess that's what makes it magical," Soni concluded.

The Numbers Speak Volumes

Exactly," Rob assured her. "So, let's revisit some gym numbers where a few fitness statistics might just apply to both *help* and *hold* . . . as well as *share* to *secure*. Twenty-nine percent of all gym members use personal trainers.[5] And forty percent enroll in gym classes to work out together."[6]

"You might recall the message from our website that supports this," Ester said, having pulled it up on her iPad for Soni to view.

---

[5] Statista, 2021

[6] https://the conversation.com

Soni read it to herself. *If you are someone who operates better in a group setting, our group training services might be perfect for you. Our trainers can handle several clients at a time, ensuring that everyone gets the attention they need and that the workout remains challenging. This is an excellent way to stay accountable and to make friends with people who have the same fitness goals!*

"Allow me to share a few more facts," Rob interjected. "Research shows that being physically active can improve one's brain health and also help manage weight. In addition, it can reduce the risk of disease, strengthen muscles and bones, and improve one's ability to do everyday activities.[7] Ester and I would like to believe that most people are aware of at least a few of these benefits."

"Yet, eighty percent of adults,"[8] Ester confessed, "do *not* meet the minimum guidelines for both aerobic and muscle-strengthening activities. And only nineteen percent of the U.S. population have a gym membership."[9]

"But just because they have one, doesn't mean they use it," Rob confided. "Sadly, eight of ten people who join a gym in January quit before the end of spring.[10] Of those who do keep their memberships for the year, only eighteen percent of those members go to their gym regularly."[11]

---

[7] https://www.health.harvard.edu/mind-and-mood/a-workout-for-your-brain

[8] Office of Disease Prevention and Health Promotion https://odphp.health.gov

[9] https://wod.guru/blog/managing-a-gym/

[10] https://www.glofox.com/blog/6-new-years-resolution-gym-statistics-you-need-to-know/

[11]https://thehustle.co/news/people-are-actually-using-their-gym-memberships-that-s-a-prob

Soni began computing the numbers. "So, if I take eighteen percent . . . the number of those who attend . . . of the nineteen percent . . . the number who have memberships, I get . . . "

Ester politely interrupted, "Less than three-and-one-half percent. We've already done the math."

"That's pathetic!" Soni offered. "In summary, several things stand out. One would think that most people know they would benefit from what is offered at a gym, but have chosen not to get a membership. Their loss."

"A most accurate statement."

"Then, a handful do join, and for a brief time, reap the benefits. Yet, in no time, they return to their old ways and eventually quit. They, too, lose, just more slowly."

"Yes, again."

"Lastly, a select few not only *see* the value in what is offered, but more importantly, *do* something about it. They *jump*. They *attend*. They are *self*-managed. And as a result, they benefit immensely from it."

"Comparing these numbers to our conversation from the other night, what did you just describe?" Ester quizzed.

"Our sales team," Soni responded with a dejected look.

"And the statistics just quoted in the fitness industry closely match the makeup of your groups."

"They do, Ester. The majority of our salespeople recognize they would benefit from the knowledge they gained from their training, but have chosen not to apply it. A handful are using bits and pieces. At best, they are just doing okay, at least for a while. Lastly, a select few are *doing* what they have been trained to do and are excelling. And now I realize why. It's because they are *self*-managed!"

"Rolly informed us this is the case with the majority of people, including the majority of teams, in every industry. It certainly was for us. They are all being managed, instead of being taught how to become *self*-managed."

Seek and Ye Shall Find

That's sad," Soni confessed. "So, back to the reason the three of you met. I am curious if Rolly explained what led him to pursue help for accountability issues from within the health and fitness industry?"

Ester stepped away for a moment as Rob responded, "Yes, ma'am, we were surprised by the request. And yes, Rolly did share how that came about. He said the idea was hatched—his words, not ours—by simply listening to others."

"Hatched!" Soni smirked. "Sounds just like him. When it comes to listening, Rolly is the best. I shared with my team that of his many admirable qualities, he has three that truly stand out: a *curious* mind . . . a *listening* ear . . . and an *open* heart. In my book, you cannot go wrong with that combination."

"Well, I sincerely thank you for that compliment, my dear!" Rolly stated, catching Soni totally by surprise. "Speaking of books, that would have been a good message for **S.M.I.L.E.**"

Soni quickly scanned the stage to locate her friend. "Rolly, where are you? I didn't notice you come in. I can hear you, but this time I *can't* find you."

Having placed a FaceTime call with Rolly, Ester reappeared with him on her iPad. "He is right here, Soni. Rolly felt you would ask this question, and the three of us agreed it would be best if he explained." She addressed her iPad and continued, "Rolly, the stage has been set for you. Except this time, Soni is posing the questions."

"I like that little twist, Ester. And Soni, before I respond, have you enjoyed your time with Ester and Rob?"

"Have I ever. Thanks to them, I see the obvious parallels between those who *stand out* in the business world and those who *work out* in the gym."

Rolly smiled. "I like the way you put that."

"Thank you, sir. I like the way you tied the Keys to *self*-management to the Six Honest Serving Men. The images were so easy to picture and remember." She paused to give Rolly a wink. "And an extra special thanks for reading *Snow White* to your little ones. The visual of the magic mirrors on the walls was *so* helpful!"

"That is what we were hoping for, Soni. Now, to your question. Some time back, I acquired two partners—former students I've known and trusted—who help teach my different programs. It was time for them to get in on the fun. Plus, it would free me up to find ways to enhance the content, improve the results, and even add new programs."

"Good for them!" Soni proclaimed. "And good for you!"

"Thank you, ma'am. These partners observed that with every out-of-town group, one or two students, without fail, would get up earlier than the others to perform some physical exercise: walking, jogging, calisthenics, yoga, swimming, or weightlifting."

"If jumping to conclusions, running one's mouth, dodging responsibility, and pushing one's luck qualify, I believe

I was that person in my group!" Soni exclaimed with another wink. The three burst into raucous laughter at her remark.

"Soni, you've always been a piece of work, and still are!" Rolly shouted. "Back to the answer. They also noticed that these individuals were closely monitoring their diet, including what they ate, how much they ate, and how much they drank. At some point, they were asked if they were engaged in a health or fitness regimen back home. When they confirmed they were, the obvious question was why they were not tempted just to let themselves go while away."

"I loved their curiosity, too, Rolly."

"As did I. And I loved what they learned. Their responses boiled down to two things: control and accountability. Regardless of whether they used the words, they all felt they were in control. And with control came accountability. They were in control *and* accountable for their actions."

Soni confided, "We discussed control just a bit ago."

"I am not surprised. That is when I began exploring the world of health and fitness. Just think about it. Why would people *who* have no manager telling them *what* to do, *where* to do it, *why* to do it, *when* to do it, and *how* to do it, manage to do so on their own? The answer was obvious. They were *self*-managed. So, I . . ."

Soni politely interrupted, "May I, Rolly?" She received a go-ahead nod from her feathered friend. "So, you needed a way to tie everything together—something that would contain the questions they almost certainly would have considered. And that way was Rudyard Kipling's poem."

"Very good. Once I began my research, it became apparent that the first Five Keys would provide the commonality as to what prompted people to *decide* to pay their own hard-earned money to join a gym. I just needed that confirmed."

Rob interjected, "And we did that during Rolly's visit."

"But it was the Sixth Key of **Who**," Ester said, "that led us *all* to accountability . . . to actually *doing.* The members who show up are *doers.* They *jump.* They are *accountable.* They are *self*-managed, just like the individuals Rolly's partners observed in their classes."

"I am pleased to say that Ester and I now use these Keys and our Six Serving Men with *all* our new members. For those who are already *self*-managed, learning about it provides a better understanding and appreciation for their approach. As for the majority who are not . . . well, they relish the thought of learning how to *self*-manage their health and fitness needs to get the results they're paying for."

"In addition, Rob and I are reaching out to reconnect with those members who have not been attending, who have demonstrated by their actions that they are not *self*-managed. The Keys and our Six Serving Men are now prompting them to *show* up . . . to *jump* . . . to *do* . . . to become *self*-managed. And with each success, Rob and I are fulfilling our purpose of helping them achieve their goals. We are proud of that."

"As you should be, Ester," Soni agreed.

"What we are *most* proud of," Rob shared, "is that we let go of the strings that were controlling our staff and have replaced them with the Keys to *self*-management."

Ester agreed. "We welcome the thought of having helped our team get where they want to be."

The Lighting of a Fire

I sincerely thank all of you for helping me get closer to where I want to be with my team," Soni stated. She turned to address Rolly. "One last question, sir. Thanks to the simplicity of the Keys and the doors opened by the Six Serving Men, I have a basic understanding of the role they play in helping people to become *self*-managed, certainly in the gym."

"That's comforting to know."

"And I acknowledge I have a lot still to learn from the individuals you are about to introduce me to in how to apply this to *my* world. But what will actually motivate those on our team who are not *self*-managed, including those who may not even be inclined to become *self*-managed, to want to adopt this approach? In **S.M.I.L.E.**, Sherri's students gave her a plaque that read . . .

Education is not the filling of a pail,
but the lighting of a fire!

No question, I will be educating them—I have a lot to pour into that pail. But, more importantly, what is going to light a fire under my people who may need a fire lit?"

"That is *THE* question, Soni. Under normal circumstances, that answer would be revealed during one of our upcoming ***Self*-Management Retreats**—the first of which is scheduled for next month."

Soni patted her abdomen. "Pardon the pun, but I take it these must be *ab*-normal circumstances?" Everyone chuckled at her wit.

"Yes, ma'am. What you have experienced today was *ab*normal—abnormal in that you would typically learn about *all* of this by attending a **Retreat**."

Soni held up her portfolio. "Is that where I would have received this little 'gift' that I also need to thank you for?"

"Thanks to Ester and Rob, it is now. When they described it, we agreed it needed to become the one we use going forward. And you're welcome. Since these **Retreats** are all booked well into next year—and the fact that you are one of my absolute best students ever—I . . . "

"And *favorite*?" Soni playfully interjected.

"Yes, ma'am," Rolly responded as he rolled his eyes, "and favorite, I chose to make an exception. Thanks to Ester and Rob being both flexible and accommodating, as are the other folks I have already contacted, you get to experience what you would learn at a **Retreat** directly from the sources. And much sooner, I might add. As for *THE* answer to your question, I am confident Ester and Rob would recommend you discover it from two powerhouse women who have been 'living' it for quite some time."

Ester excitedly exclaimed, "If you are referring to Karen Cooper and Vicky Noufal, they are *precisely* from whom she needs to learn it. Following your initial visit here, the phone conversations you arranged with them gave us the necessary tools to help begin to bring the Six Keys and Serving Men to life."

Rob added, "We appreciated your offer to have us meet with them in person. We couldn't get away at the time."

"But I can!" Soni excitedly proclaimed. "Rolly, if you were here in person . . . excuse me . . . in parrot, I'd hug your sweet little neck." Everyone laughed again. "Just so you know, I have already received Holly's blessing to devote as much time as needed to this effort, including any travel requirements necessary. I am ready to pack my bags when I get home this evening. When and where am I headed?"

"Northern Virginia, Tuesday morning. Along with providing you with *THE* answer to your question, Karen and Vicky will focus on the **What** and **Where** Keys and the doors these first two Serving Men open. Wednesday morning, you will be flying to San Antonio to meet with Cheri Bass and Craig Owen for the **Why** and **When** Keys."

"Another Sherri, like in **S.M.I.L.E.**," Soni stated.

"Yes, ma'am," Rolly answered. "Except this one is spelled with a 'C' instead of an 'S.' And Thursday afternoon, you will be in Phoenix, where you will conclude the week with Hal Looney, Rick Andreen, and Tiffany Torgan. They will address the final Keys of **How** and **Who**. You will return home Friday. We will discuss details in a bit when you call me on your way home."

"How exciting. I'm looking forward to meeting everyone, starting with Karen and Vicky.

"And they are most excited to meet you."

"You are a blessing, my friend," Soni confided. She blew Rolly a farewell kiss.

Rolly pretended to catch it and sent one of his own. "I am the one who is blessed with friends like you, everyone you are about to meet, and of course . . . Ester and Rob. Goodbye to all of you."

"It was our pleasure," Ester exclaimed as she ended the call and turned to address Soni. "Rob and I hope it has been a good day for you. It certainly has been for us."

"It has been an unbelievable day for me. As for questions, could I get a few more of your business cards before I leave? I know lots of folks I'd like to refer your way."

"That's a given, and will be greatly appreciated," Rob reassured her. "Another given is a need for a restroom break. Let's meet back at the front desk afterwards. The restrooms are just down the hallway from there."

When she returned to the front desk, Soni was pleasantly surprised when offered a Big Tex Gym bag. "Ester and I put a little 'care package' together so you won't forget us."

Inside, she found an assortment of monogrammed workout apparel, along with an envelope containing business cards. "You and Ester are too much. These tops are cute! I can wear them to promote your business. And thanks for the cards, too. Aside from the physical gifts you have given me, the gift of wisdom on how I can begin helping my team become *self*-managed is the best of all. How can I ever repay you?"

"You already have," Ester answered. "Rob and I are scheduled to speak at the upcoming ***Self*-Management Retreats**. We are so excited and honored."

"That's an understatement," Rob added. "Allowing us the opportunity today to hone our skills in delivering this message was most beneficial."

"I'm glad I could help. And there's no way I'm forgetting you and what I've experienced today," Soni replied. "By the way, I must share that I'm leaving here with a third gift."

"A third?" Rob questioned. Ester looked puzzled, too.

"Yes, sir. A gift of inspiration. This visit has inspired me to renew my gym membership and take better care of myself."

Ester smiled. "Thank you for sharing that. You just made our day, Soni."

Rob and Ester walked Soni to her car, where they hugged goodbye. Being the consummate gentleman, Rob opened her car door as Ester handed her a cold beverage in a Big Tex Gym koozie. "I know how you like this drink. One cool tea to-go for one cool *self*-managed lady *on* the go."

"Thank you both for being who you are. I love y'all dearly!" Soni offered with a beaming smile.

"We love you, too," Ester and Rob replied in unison. "And please tell Karen and Vicky we said hello. They are the best."

"You can count on it."

Section 3:
THE KEYS TO HISTORY

Three of a Kind

Soni arrived early for her mid-afternoon meeting with Karen and Vicky, having secured a standby seat on a direct flight to Arlington, Virginia. After a ten-minute Uber ride to Old Town Alexandria, she dropped her carry-on at her Airbnb. With the weather ideal, she chose to get in her exercise for the day by taking a walk along the Potomac River waterfront of the old trans-Atlantic seaport. Established in 1749, the town was bursting with historic charm.

Enjoying the sights and sounds, she followed the GPS directions along the cobblestone streets, lined with eighteenth-century townhouses, to her meeting destination . . . Gadsby's Tavern—home to fine dining since 1770.

Soni was greeted by a hostess dressed in period attire and escorted to an elegant colonial dining room reserved for their meeting. Taking a glass of water from a side table stocked with beverages, she selected a seat at a mahogany table facing an ornate fireplace. As she soaked in the ambiance of this treasured establishment, she connected her iPad to the Internet and tapped the link to Karen's website she had just received from Rolly. She was intrigued by the name: empoweringwomeninrealestate.com. She loved the message from the heading even more as she read to herself:

WHAT WE DO

Helping women grow a successful real estate business without sacrificing their quality of life.

How refreshing, she thought. *Someone focused on others. I haven't even met this lady, and I already love her.* She continued reading as if Karen were speaking to her.

Hi, I'm Karen! In 2014, I found myself feeling lonely and depressed in my business. I'd spent ten years as a top-producing Realtor® with three kids under ten, and I was BURNED OUT ... so I accepted a position as a managing broker, thinking it would solve all my problems (spoiler alert: it didn't). Nearly two years in, and I felt like I was moving further and further away from myself, craving connection, inspiration, and a tribe of women who would "get it."

Enter, Empowering Women in Real Estate®. What started as a shower idea (aren't those the best ones?) for a Facebook community all those years ago has turned into what you see here ... a podcast, Monthly Meet Ups throughout the US and Canada, a top-notch annual conference, and our signature Inner Circle program. That Facebook community? It's going strong with many tens of thousands of women and is one of the greatest blessings of my life.

Soni sighed. *What a woman. What a vision. And what a radiant smile in every picture,* she noted as she scrolled through the site. *If Vicky is anything like Karen, I'm in for quite an experience. I wonder if I can learn a little about Vicky and how the two met.* As she continued to scroll, she noticed a fun photo of Karen and a lady at the beach, both wearing bandanas and smiling as they embraced. "Could this be Vicky?" she uttered aloud.

Having lost herself in the moment, Soni was unaware that Karen and Vicky had entered the room and were now standing directly behind her. Karen was peering over Soni's shoulder. She playfully whispered, "Sure looks like her to me."

Startled, Soni jumped to her feet and turned to find the two had struck the same pose from the photograph. "Oh, my," she stammered, "I didn't hear you come in. I got here early in hopes of learning a little about the two of you. Please forgive me for not greeting both of you properly."

"There's nothing to forgive," Vicky assured her with a big smile. "We also love folks who get immersed in what they do. And, as you can tell, we love being early, too."

"We also love to update old photos," Karen added. "Would you care to help recreate our little hug with you joining us?"

Soni blushed. "I would be honored."

After introducing themselves, Karen took a selfie of the three, grinning from ear to ear. As she revealed the picture, she proudly exclaimed, "Now that's the proper way to begin a new friendship: smiles, a hug, and a selfie."

"Soni, with your permission, might we include it on the website?" Vicky asked. "And if I might add, your Big Tex Gym shirt is way cool and perfect for the mood."

"Permission granted, Vicky," Soni replied. "It's a gift from Ester and Rob. Rolly suggested this was a more casual meeting, so I packed light."

"He shared the same with us, which is why we *dressed* light —jeans and sandals instead of dresses and heels. We also lightened our schedule by forwarding our calls and messages to our team. We're yours for the afternoon and evening."

Soni took their cue to switch her phone to "Respectful Mode."

"Thank you. By the way, Ester and Rob said hello."

"They're a darling couple," Karen replied. "We love that you're promoting their business. Vicky and I have built our business through referrals and word of mouth."

"That's impressive, Karen. For all the help they've given me, they deserve to be promoted. It also helps that their shirts are extremely comfortable. And, as Vicky pointed out . . . look cool, too!"

As everyone took a seat, Karen remarked, "We enjoy comfort and cool. We also enjoy welcoming folks with a little gift with our official state slogan, 'Virginia is for Lovers.' " Karen reached into her handbag to offer Soni a baseball cap and a T-shirt with that logo on it.

"We love mountains, rivers, beaches, wine, and history," Vicky detailed. "And an *occasional* Texan," she subtly winked. The three chuckled.

"I love all those," Soni replied. "And thank you for the cap and shirt. I can wear them on my trip to Texas tomorrow, where I'll be making two new friends. Texas happens to be 'The Friendship State.' We love rodeos, football, dance halls, barbecue, and margaritas. And we've been known to welcome an *occasional* Virginian our way," she playfully added. "Come to think of it, Sam Houston—one of the heroes of the Texas Revolution and the first president of the Republic of Texas—was a native Virginian."

"We love all those things—especially someone who knows their history."

Karen nodded. "Most of all, I can tell we love you already."

Soni became captivated by the charisma of these two women. "Same here. You both are so friendly, so much fun, so alive. How long have you been friends?"

"We thank you for the compliment," Karen responded. "Since I'm the numbers gal in our duo, I'd best answer that. We met nineteen years ago on the first team we were part of at a national brokerage. I'd been there three years before Vicky was hired as a new agent and assigned to shadow or help me. Truth is, with her background in business planning, strategy, and marketing innovation, I could have easily been assigned to shadow *her*." She reached out to squeeze Vicky's hand. "Now, we *are* each other's shadow! We do everything together. As part of her training, she covered for me during my second pregnancy and maternity leave. We started as colleagues, then became friends, then business partners, and now . . . "

Vicky politely interrupted, "And now . . . we are family. And when I say family, I mean *family*! I love this lady and could not imagine my life without her." Her voice began to tremble as tears welled in her eyes. "Karen was there for me and my three sons when I lost my husband, their father, to pancreatic cancer seven years ago. She's been our rock." With everyone now in tears, Vicky rushed to get tissues from the side table to share with Karen and Soni.

"Thank you for the tissue. You've been my rock as well." Then Karen turned toward Soni. "Vicky helped me battle breast tumor recurrences that have required no less than ten surgeries and thirty radiation treatments over the past sixteen years. She always stepped in for me when I was physically, mentally, or emotionally unable to care for our team and families we work with in the way we must." Karen wiped more tears from her eyes as the two stood to hug once more.

Reading the moment, Soni stood and placed her right foot on her chair to reveal the anklet she wore. "I don't share this with everyone, but you two likely know what this represents."

Karen recognized it immediately. "It's a 'Circle of Hope' for breast cancer survivors. You, too, Soni?"

"Me, too, Karen," she sighed as she embraced her fellow combatant. "I'm two years in recovery after multiple surgeries." Vicky joined the hug as all three wiped away tears.

Vicky sensed the need to lighten the mood. "I must say, I don't recall when I've been this active just meeting someone. Walking in, posing for pictures, hugging, sitting, wiping tears, running for tissues, sitting again, standing again, hugging again, and wiping more tears. For Pete's sake, I feel like a jack-in-the-box that's wound too tight. Can we all sit down and get back to smiling and laughing?" Everyone laughed . . . and smiled . . . and sat back down.

"Thank you, Vicky," Soni remarked. "We needed that." She turned to address Karen. "I must ask, did challenges like these—the trials and tribulations it seems we women are forever dealing with—motivate you to found *Empowering Women in Real Estate*?"

"They did, along with the lack of respect and recognition women seldom receive, considering the many roles we play in a stressful and demanding profession. A profession, I might add, that far too often jeopardizes our quality of life."

Founding Fathers

"Amen to *all* that!" Soni emphatically agreed. She paused for a moment, weighing what she was about to say. "Karen, I've only known you a few minutes, but you impress me as someone who does nothing by accident. I say that because, on my walk from my Airbnb, I noticed several restaurants you could have chosen for our meeting. I have a feeling this topic of empowering women, along with the **What** and **Where** Keys and their Serving Men we're here to discuss, has something to do with you selecting Gadsby's Tavern."

"You're correct on both accounts, Soni. Let's begin with **What** and **Where**. As you might appreciate, there's a lot of history in this area."

"I agree. Several years back, my husband and I, along with our two kids, vacationed in D.C. We visited the Smithsonian, the National Cathedral, Arlington Cemetery, and most of the monuments, including our nation's capital. We were exhausted by the end of our trip. But we didn't visit Gadsby's. It didn't show up on any of the brochures or 'must-see' places to visit."

"That's unfortunate since most historians feel *no* building in our nation's history was more intimately associated with our struggle for independence than this tavern. At that time, it was *the* center of political, social, and cultural life."

"Within these walls," Vicky divulged, "the majority of our Founding Fathers—men who championed American independence—enjoyed its welcoming hospitality. Many of the conversations and decisions made in this very room would begin to shape our destiny and forever change the world."

Again, Soni glanced at her surroundings. "That sends chills down my spine knowing much of it began right here."

"It still does ours. And when you think about it, the basic principle behind *all* this—their desire to gain independence from British rule—was simply a yearning to become *self*-managed. They wanted to be able to manage themselves."

"I've never made that association," Soni acknowledged. "However, I suppose that's precisely what it was about."

"From that perspective," Karen shared, "it's easy to see the connection of our Six Serving Men and their Keys to *self*-management, to what occurred in the American Revolution. It began with them being dissatisfied with their current situation in the British colonies . . . as subjects . . . of the British Crown. They longed instead to become citizens . . . in independent states . . . of a sovereign nation."

"The first Two Keys: **What** and **Where**."

"Exactly, Soni! They didn't like **What** their current situation was, and they knew **Where** they wanted to be. From there, they likely made a list that could stretch from here to Boston Harbor as to **Why** they wanted to be there."

"Taxation without representation," Vicky speculated, "would have been high on that list. The reason **Why** an entire cargo of tea was tossed into that harbor in 1773—the famous Boston Tea Party."

"**When** they wanted this to happen would have been next," Karen reasoned.

"I'm guessing that's where July 4th of 1776 might have come into play . . . Independence Day."

"Excellent, Soni. Which would have been followed by **How** they planned to get there. To give us a taste of just how vitally important this part was, if you will google *Revolutionary War Strategy* on your iPad, we'll read the first part of an article from *American Battlefield Trust*."

By the time Karen and Vicky could retrieve a refreshment from the side table, Soni had it pulled up. "Since I'm holding the iPad, it would be my pleasure to read it . . .

The American strategy was about obtaining legitimacy on an international level. While the Declaration of Independence was written to spell out American ideals and principles, its main purpose was to flash a rescue beacon to the international world. As the former colonies sought to throw off the yoke of British authority, there remained the real chance that no other country would look upon them as anything more than unruly British subjects. This is precisely what the British wanted, and what the Patriot leaders feared. Courting foreign nations to recognize the United States as a sovereign nation was the main goal of diplomats Benjamin Franklin and John Adams. From a diplomatic stance, without foreign assistance, the United States stood little chance of achieving true independence.

"Thank you, Soni. You can stop there," Karen instructed. "In addition, volunteers had to be recruited and trained, spy networks developed, tactics formulated on when and where to engage the British army in skirmishes, battle plans drawn, along with a multitude of other details—all critical elements of **How**."

"Which brings us to **Who** would help and hold them accountable," Vicky reasoned. "The fact that we're here today tells us those who fought for this cause were able to *hold* themselves accountable. But if you would repeat the last sentence of what you just read, we'll be reminded of how important the *help* was that they received."

Sensing the gravity of what she was about to reread, Soni spoke with a patriotic fervor this time around. ***"From a diplomatic stance, without foreign assistance, the United States stood little chance of achieving true independence."***

"Well done, Soni. You deserve an Oscar for that!"

Soni smiled and placed one arm across her waist, and bent slightly to take a bow. "I was honored."

"And Ben Franklin, John Adams, and the remaining Founding Fathers were honored to receive that help. It came from three nations: Spain, France, and the Netherlands. Historians agree that without their help, they would never have gained their independence. At least not then."

"It turns out," Karen surmised, "that our Founding Fathers benefited immensely from the services of our Six Serving Men and the Keys they possessed!"

"Karen and I are willing to bet that if we took the time to explore it, we would discover that our Sam Houston and the other heroes of the *Texas* Revolution also benefited from their services as well."

The ***Self***-Management Model

"Now that you mention it, I would have to agree," Soni confessed. She paused for a moment to process everything she had just experienced. "In reality, it would appear that what Rolly has introduced to us—the Keys to *self*-management and our Six Serving Men—is nothing new. It was one thing for Rolly to connect this to the members in the health and fitness world who were *self*-managed. But to go back

250 years to the American Revolution . . . well, that's something else entirely!"

"We agree," Karen confided. "But in all likelihood, this ***Self*-Management Model**, as Vicky and I have coined it, could likely be traced back much further than that."

"It's similar to gravity," Vicky proposed. "It's been around a long time, too. History tells us it was a *well-known* phenomenon in early civilizations. It just was not *well understood.* Let's face it, apples were falling from trees long before Englishman Isaac Newton took note of it a hundred years before the Revolutionary War. Yet, he's given credit for 'discovering' gravity. Not to discount the importance of his work, but what he did was help us better *understand* it."

"I like that," Soni declared.

"Thank you. When Vicky and I discussed the term ***Self*-Management Model** with Rolly, he liked it and encouraged us to use it as a way to both signify and simplify its meaning. It truly is a model—a way of *understanding* how one manages to become *self*-managed."

"Turns out that over the years, Karen and I have applied it to help tens of thousands of women become *self*-managed, without knowing we were using it. We just needed Rolly to reveal the model to us and the world. Apparently, it was always there."

"What you're saying is it took a birdbrain for the rest of us to see it!" Soni surmised. Karen and Vicky roared at her comment. Soni even laughed.

"We didn't see that one coming!" Vicky declared, still laughing. "The truth is, you're correct. Speaking of revolutions, this simple model has the potential to revolutionize the business world. By using it, managers can stop managing their subjects and free them to *self*-manage themselves."

"Oh, my, I like what you just said. Just please don't tell Rolly what I just said, okay?" Soni sheepishly requested.

Karen put her index finger to her lips. "It's our little secret," she promised.

Founding Mothers

So, Karen," Soni inquired, "what is the connection with empowering women to Gadsby's?"

"It has to do with Abigail Adams, the wife of our second president, John Adams."

"*The* same diplomat . . . Founding Father John Adams, whom I just read about?"

"*The* very same John Adams. Abigail enjoyed dining here with her husband. And in the 2004 book *Founding Mothers: The Women Who Raised Our Nation*, award-winning author, journalist, and historian Cokie Roberts considers Abigail Adams one of our Founding Mothers."

"I like Abigail and Cokie already."

"Us, too. We hear a lot about 'influencers' today. Cokie tells us that Abigail was a political influencer in her day, writing some twelve hundred letters to her husband during the countless times they were apart. Most were filled with intellectual discussions on government and politics. According to Cokie, Abigail famously wrote a letter to her husband in March 1776, while he was attending the Continental Congress in Philadelphia. In it, she reminded him that in the new form of government being established, he should, and I quote,

'Remember the ladies and be more generous and favorable to them than your ancestors, or they too, would foment a revolution of their own.' "

Vicky recalled, "Cokie writes that she was also a strong advocate for women's property rights. Abigail was convinced that women should not submit to laws not made in their interest. Nor should they be content with the simple role of being companions to their husbands. She believed women should educate themselves and be recognized for their intellectual capabilities. In doing so, she felt they could help guide and influence the lives of their children *and* husbands."

"What an incredible woman," Soni exclaimed. "It's obvious Abigail was a strong believer in empowering women."

"Bingo. Thus, the connection with Karen's idea in the shower she talks about on our website—the founding of *Empowering Women in Real Estate.* Oh, before we move on, there's one more connection to make. Abigail was the proud mother of six children." Vicky reached for Soni's hand and leaned in. "Sadly, in 1813, she lost her oldest daughter, Nabby, to breast cancer. Nabby was only forty-eight," she softly whispered.

Soni teared up. "Bless her heart. That breaks *my* heart. What an inspiring wife, mother, and woman."

"A Pulitzer Prize-winning historian, Joseph Ellis—another of the nation's foremost scholars of American history—must have felt the same. He called Abigail Adams one of the most extraordinary women in American history."

Section 4:
WHAT AND WHERE

An Empowering Perspective

"Now to *THE* question," Vicky began, "regarding what would light a fire under your people to *want* to become *self*-managed. Let's begin with two questions for you. At any time, did you, Rolly, Ester, or Rob discuss the importance of perspective?"

"Yes, ma'am. And more than once, I might add."

"And was control also discussed, with the consensus that most *self*-managed people want to be in control of their lives?"

"Affirmative, and we all agreed on that position."

"Even better. Returning to perspective, Soni, another way to look at *self*-management, which involves wanting to be in control, is the concept of *empowerment.* Did you by chance bring the portfolio we were told you received?"

"I did," Soni responded as she removed it from her handbag and proudly placed it on the table. "And I love it!"

"Ditto from us. That's nice!" Karen remarked. She removed a manila folder from her handbag and gave Soni a page from it. "You'll notice we printed Wikipedia's definition of empowerment. I should mention that it was Vicky's idea to print it on parchment paper and use an Old English font so it would appear to come from that time in history. She's the *creative* one."

Vicky grinned. "It was Karen's idea to have it laminated so it would be protected and three-hole punched. She's the *practical* one." Everyone laughed.

"You two are something else. And thanks to both of you for going above and beyond."

"It was our pleasure," Karen responded. "The definition is to remind us of the purpose of the Keys to *self*-management and our Six Serving Men. See if these words provide you with *THE* answer to what will light a fire under your people. You're welcome to read it aloud, Soni."

"Empowerment: to make (someone) stronger and more confident, especially in controlling their life and claiming their rights."

After pausing to let the meaning sink in, Soni reread it. "Empowerment: to make someone *stronger* and more *confident* . . . especially in controlling *their* life and claiming *their* rights. All I can say is thank you for sharing this! Over the years, I must have heard and used this word a thousand times. But now I see that I never truly understood its meaning. It's no wonder those who are *self*-managed enjoy the feeling of control. They *are* free—free to *control* their lives and claim their rights. They are *empowered.* And from a manager's perspective, the possibility of helping members of your team become stronger and more confident—to control *their* life and claim *their* rights—makes what we do more meaningful than we've ever imagined."

"That's what *Empowering Women in Real Estate* is all about," Vicky declared. "When we first met Rolly and he discovered Karen's passion—the idea of not only *empowering* others but *promoting* it—he instantly knew he'd found the catalyst that would cause those not *self*-managed to want to become so."

"As for managers," Karen speculated, "it would be the same spark for them to want to help their team learn how to become *self*-managed. Empowerment offers control, and *self*-management is how we help others get there!"

"Which is why I'm here. I'm curious how that first meeting with Rolly came about."

"Mike Mallott, a dear friend and highly esteemed home inspector we use in our market, gave us a copy of **S.M.I.L.E.** We knew the moment we read it, we had to meet Rolly—and we're forever grateful to Mike for making that introduction."

"I know Rolly feels the same way," Soni confided as she filed the page behind the tab she had labeled 'Virginia Visit.' "

"Before we move on," Vicky suggested, "you might examine the back side of that page where you'll discover a special surprise Rolly asked us to put together. It combines the images of the Six Keys . . . with the doors they unlock . . . along with the term we coined . . . *plus* the 'Empowerment' answer you'd been searching for."

"Oh, there's one little thing Vicky left out. It's the contribution you made that we just added yesterday—the one initiated with the question you asked Rolly. Let's see if you can find it," Karen teased.

Soni excitedly flipped to the other side . . .

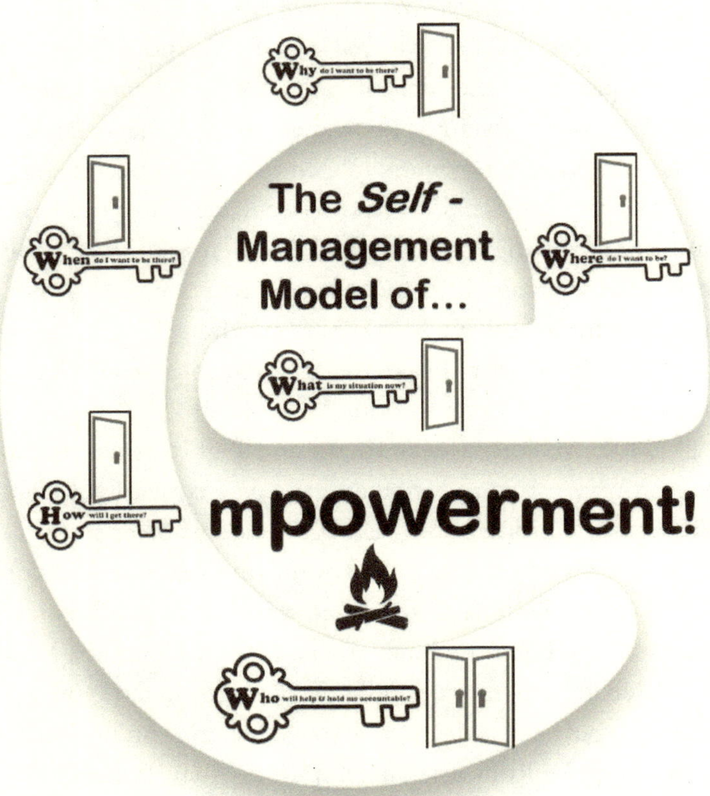

Soni perused the image. "This is *so* creative! I see the Keys . . . the doors . . . the title of the model . . . all embedded in the **'e'** in 'empowerment.' I love *everything* about this! But Vicky didn't mention the fire. Is that *my* contribution, Karen?" Soni proudly assumed.

"It is, Soni. When Rolly told us you referenced Sherri's plaque in hopes of learning what would light a fire under your people, it was obvious to all that we needed to find a symbol for it, plus an appropriate place to put it."

"And we did," Vicky acknowledged, "right under the enlarged font emphasizing the *power* in empowerment. It's as if it's providing *firepower* to the meaning of empowerment."

"When we emailed this to Rolly to get his approval, he was so pleased that he chose it as the official logo of the ***Self-*** **Management Program.**"

"Awww . . . now I'm really *fired up* with excitement!" Soni beamed.

Birds of a Feather

Indeed, we are, too," Vicky confirmed. "And Karen and I are excited to proceed to the details of the **What** and **Where** Keys and their Serving Men. You realize in doing so, we'll also touch lightly on the other Keys and their Serving Men as well."

"I anticipated you would have to since all are connected in some way—dependent on one another."

"That they are. So, Karen and I need to know if you want the *Reader's Digest* version—short and sweet? Or would you prefer the unabridged novel? We ask because there's a lot we're prepared to cover."

"Thank you for asking," Soni graciously answered. "I choose the latter. I've got a lot to learn."

"Novel it is, Soni. We expected that choice. Let's begin by discussing four commonalities you have with our women, or our *tribe,* as we affectionately call them."

Soni addressed Karen with admiration. "It appears you *did* find your 'tribe of women who would *get* it.' "

"Did I ever! And they are special. Our team of fifty-five amazing women and moms consists primarily of seasoned agents with an average of nine years of experience in the business. They have enjoyed a high level of production, with each averaging over ten million dollars in sales volume per year, and many exceeding that number. Despite their success, they aim to improve even further. And they come to us for help and mentoring to take their performance to another level."

"That's impressive . . . and inspiring."

"It is," Vicky agreed, "as is your success story that Rolly shared. You also come with a great deal of experience and success. He bragged about your climb up the corporate ladder to eventually running a homebuilding division. That's quite an accomplishment. Congratulations!"

"Thank you. I just want to get better so I can help our team get better and *do* better."

"So, we have the first three commonalities covered," Karen remarked, "experienced, successful, and a desire to get better. The last commonality may prove the most relevant for what we're about to discuss. You, as well as many of the women in our tribe, come from the corporate world. Come to think of it, quite a few from homebuilding."

"That doesn't surprise me. Quite a number I've sold with, and others on my team, have done so."

"They tell us a business plan in that world drives everything. That's understandable; they're a business. Depending on the business, that plan determines the goals: number of sales to make, widgets produced, memberships sold, contracts procured, units leased, services provided, etc."

"From there," Vicky added, "they tell us management then communicates those numbers, those performance goals, to their team. In addition, they determine when they are to be met, to what standards, the activities performed to achieve them, as well as the work hours required."

"Welcome to my world," Soni sighed. "We're pretty good at pulling strings."

"That we've been told," Karen agreed. "They also shared that what's most frustrating is that they seldom, if ever, had any input into that plan. Worse yet, they were then micromanaged by someone always looking over their shoulder, even when they were exceeding their goals. Year after year, it was the same process: wash-rinse-repeat, wash-rinse-repeat. Over time, this does not wear well on the human psyche. They felt encumbered, not empowered."

"Which is why," Vicky advised, "so many leave the corporate world and get into real estate. Here, they can be their own boss. They can set their own goals. They can determine what they want to do, when they do it, how they do it, and the amount of time they will put into it, with no limit on their income. *And* with no one standing over them."

"Which all sounds great," Karen confessed, "until you look at the failure rate of most real estate agents. Sadly, on average, nearly seventy-five percent of new agents quit within their first year.[12] That's pretty dismal."

"It is," Soni agreed. "But I'm not at all surprised by that number. We experience that in our market. I'm betting it's no coincidence this happens to be close to the same percentage

---

[12] National Association of REALTORS® (NAR®)

Ester and Rob shared regarding the number of new members who join a gym in January and quit before the end of spring."

"And chances are this dropout rate occurs for the same reason for both groups. Both are missing the Sixth Key and Serving Man, **Who**—who is necessary to help them and to hold them accountable to do what must be done."

"Here is the reason Karen and I say that: even the few who do survive that first year, who have proven to some degree to be *self*-managed, need help reaching their *full* potential."

"Which explains our tribe," Karen revealed.

"What you're saying is that you and Vicky are in their magic mirrors. On one side of the hall, you may be asked to provide the *help* they need. On the other side, your presence may be requested to *hold* them accountable to reach that next level. And for some, you may be in both mirrors."

WHAT IS MY SITUATION NOW?

That we are," Vicky nodded with a smile. "And that *help* necessitates our employing the services of the first Five Serving Men and the Keys to *self*-management they possess. We begin by learning **What** their current situation is. We focus on four areas: Business Review, Pillars, Maintenance, and Struggles."

"These sound intriguing," Soni flashed a grin.

As Soni was about to write these down, Karen handed her a stack of papers from the manila folder. "Vicky and I thought it might help if we gave you the materials to refer to what we use with our women. The page on top, titled **WHAT** IS MY SITUATION NOW? lists these four areas."

Soni filed the pages behind the previous page and noted the four areas on the first page. "How thoughtful," she smiled.

"It's our pleasure, Soni." Karen's face shone vibrantly. "However, first, it's essential to understand that what we're about to discuss is truly effective. It's not a theory. Not pie-in-the-sky. Not hopes and dreams. It's tested and proven. I've already confessed I'm a numbers person, so it's no surprise: we track *everything*. We're old school—if we can't measure it, we can't help someone *self*-manage it. So, when I tell you our team members experience an average of 184 percent growth in their business within two to three years of joining our team, you can take that number to the bank."

"And they do, literally!" Vicky confirmed.

WHAT – PAST-YEAR BUSINESS REVIEW

Karen and I are big believers that to get where you're going, you need to know where you've been. When someone joins our team, we begin by learning **What** their current situation is by conducting a thorough review of their past year's business. And it's not just the numbers in terms of sales and volume. We dig deep to understand exactly where the business came from. This provides clarity beyond emotion to allow all to understand what is working and what is not."

"The one-on-one time Vicky and I spend with each new member when they first join us, as well as during our quarterly and annual end-of-year reviews, is another important reason these women want to become part of our tribe. Soni, you might refer to the next page titled PAST-YEAR BUSINESS REVIEW." Soni turned to it.

"As you can see, before Karen and I get into the specifics, we ask that they reflect on that year as a whole and write out the answers to three questions: What was amazing? What was overwhelming? And what was disappointing?"

"I love the wisdom in this," Soni declared. "When answering what was amazing, you're asking them to celebrate the positives—what went right. They get to pat themselves on the back. Then, having them reflect on what was overwhelming encourages them to divulge areas where they might have struggled. As for disappointing? I'm guessing that sets up the discussion later of **Where** they want to be."

"You got it, all the way around," Karen confirmed. "And none of this is in any way judgmental. We want real information: total number of transactions, settlement date, was it a buy or sell transaction, sales price, commission earned, and source of sale."

"With this information, Karen and I can then determine the total number of families served, closed volume, number of buy/sell transactions, average sales price, and average commission per transaction. All this will help set goals at the **Where** Key."

"By chance, are last year's goals discussed?"

"Absolutely. Goals for transaction numbers, price range, volume, and income. We want to know which ones they reached or exceeded, and which ones they fell short on."

"You're really getting into their business," Soni noted, wide-eyed.

"That's on purpose," Karen stressed. "We want them to see this *as* their business and take *ownership* of it by understanding how it feels to do business at a much higher level. It's a combination of knowing the numbers, including their marketing and business expenses for the year, and then evaluating them. It enables us to fulfill our goal, our purpose of empowering them. We also have more questions on the back of the page. What business lessons did they learn? What did they do best? What did they learn about themselves? What could they have done differently? If this coming year's business were a repeat of last year, would they be happy?"

"Wow, y'all are extremely thorough," Soni remarked.

WHAT – PILLARS

Thanks," Karen said. "The source of sale mentioned earlier takes us to the page titled PILLARS." Soni turned to it.

Vicky began, "Just as pillars are used in construction to support a structure, we use them as a metaphor to help our women visualize what supports their business. Pillars represent sources of leads—where their business comes from for both listings and sales."

"Like Internet, Realtor, referral, self-originated, and walk-ins that we use?" Soni asked.

"Exactly," Karen agreed. "Except, we identify more. We believe it's essential that they are aware of all possible sources for business opportunities. We try to help them envision that everyone they meet, everywhere they go, they are presented with opportunities for potential business from all the people they know, as well as new people they come in contact with."

"Karen, you realize you just described the John Norris philosophy from the ***M*** in **S.M.I.L.E.**," Soni stated. "John saw the opportunity to grow his business through relationships. He did so by always putting the needs and interests of others first. He practiced this with everyone he knew, every new person he met, and every place he did business. Although new to the industry, John transformed a struggling new home neighborhood that averaged fifteen sales per year into the company's top seller, achieving an average of 125 sales annually. And ninety percent of those were from referrals and self-originated sources."

"His story was most inspiring," Vicky recalled. "Aside from the referrals John received from his homeowners, many of his self-originated sales came from referrals from local businesses, places of worship, and even schools. In three years, I recall he received ten sales from a local dry cleaner, eight from a pie shop, five from a delicatessen, and another five from the local schools, to name a few."

"John's story certainly made an impression on you, too!" Soni realized. "If he were here, I'm confident he would tell us the strength of *his* pillars was in the depth and quality of those relationships he built with others that he worked so diligently to maintain."

"It's *all* about relationships!" Vicky emphasized. "Once identified, we have them zero in on the top three to five pillars where they've seen success."

"Vicky and I have learned that with too few pillars, they don't have enough variety to provide insulation and protection from market adjustments and irregularities. With too many, their efforts can become scattered, and they end up only scratching the surface of what could be done. In addition, we review leads and opportunities generated. From there, we can calculate conversation ratios per pillar, which indicates their effectiveness with each."

"If they keep track of the time they spend on each pillar," Vicky offered, "we can also calculate their ROTI—Return on *Time* Invested."

"I like that," Soni remarked. "Since time is the one thing we can never get back, it makes sense to know where their time is best spent. Plus, seeing it as an investment, a *limited* investment no less, ensures they make the best use of their time."

WHAT – MAINTENANCE

"Well said," Karen remarked. "Back to John. You mentioned his diligence in working to maintain the relationships he cultivated. Vicky and I want to know **What** is the current situation of the women on our team regarding staying in touch with the people associated with these pillars. How diligent are they with maintaining those relationships? The page we use to help them here is titled MAINTENANCE. It should be next." Soni flipped to that page.

"Karen and I look at maintenance—how they stay in touch—from a monthly perspective. We do so in several ways. Are they sending cards for any occasion, or no occasion at all? Do they 'Pop By' for a personal visit for those who live nearby, or quarterly for those farther away? Do they send 'Pop By' mailers for those who live too far? Do they email newsletters? Do they call or text to check in to see how they are doing?"

"This maintenance is an important part of our 'Client & Community Care Program' we created," Karen confided. "In essence, it's our marketing and nurture program."

"That's extensive," Soni eagerly approved. "I'm impressed!"

"Sadly, too often, Karen and I are *not* impressed with what we discover. We learn that many have become members of the first club James Smothers created, his 'Love 'Em and Leave 'Em' club, which we read about in the ***M*** in **S.M.I.L.E.** They love them while they are doing business with them, but leave them once that business is done."

"And much like it was with James, it's not intentional," Karen defended. "They just don't know any better. You recall that once James was introduced to John's level of serving others, he formed a new club—his 'Ambassadors' club. And in doing so, his referral business grew twelve-fold!"

"Which is just one more reason these women want to become members of your tribe," Soni remarked, "to grow *their* referral business. As I mentioned earlier, there's a reason behind everything Karen does, but I need to correct that statement. I'm now convinced there's a reason for everything *both* of you do." Soni glanced at the two. "I don't think it's an accident that *care* is the word of choice in your 'Client & Community Care Program.' You two could have opted for the names 'Follow-Up' or 'Business Development,' but you didn't. You chose *care,* and I know why."

"We *do* care. And if you care to turn to the next page titled STRUGGLES, we'll continue our discussion of caring." Soni turned to that page.

WHAT – STRUGGLES

For Vicky and me, struggles represent the crucial things in our lives that we struggle to squeeze into our day. Over the years, we've identified five areas of focus. They're printed in bold and listed in alphabetical order":

- **Family/Relationships**
- **Real Estate Business**
- **Self/Health**
- **Spirituality**
- **Wealth Creation/Money**

"When I look at these, the contrasting terms of *business* versus *personal* stand out, with the majority of your efforts focused on the personal aspects of their lives. I like that."

"Our women do, too. It tells them we care more about them as *people* than what they can *produce*."

"When you think about it," Vicky declared, "from a manager's perspective—or in our case as mentors—helping others become *self*-managed necessitates a '*People*-first—*production*-second' mindset, which mirrors the '*People*-first—*product*-second' philosophy of **S.M.I.L.E.** Both put first things first . . . *people*!"

Karen reflected on Vicky's insight. "In our youth, we all discovered the fallacy of a *production*-first philosophy from the childhood story, 'The Goose & the Golden Egg,' one of *Aesop's Fables*. You may recall learning of the foolish and greedy farmer who sacrificed the health of his goose when he lopped off its head to get to the golden eggs it produced."

"The farmer's short-sighted destruction of a valuable resource," Vicky added, "taught us we *first* have to look out for the capability of those under our care, or ourselves if we're *self*-managed. We must prioritize well-being first. With capability assured, we can *then* focus on what is produced."

"A valuable and timeless lesson," Soni proclaimed.

"Another problem can arise if there's too much focus on producing," Karen added. "You're likely familiar with the proverb, 'All work and no play makes Jack a dull boy.' "

"Ouch! That one hits close to home," Soni snickered. "My husband has used that one on me more than once."

"It can happen to us all. It simply means that without time invested in things other than work, a person can become both *bored* with what they're doing and *boring* to be around."

"Come to think of it, two other 'b' words might be applicable: *burned-out* . . . and *bitchy*!" Karen and Vicky laughed.

Karen added, "Even more reason to address these struggles up front. During our Business Plan Review and Goal Setting, which Vicky and I will address in more detail shortly, we ask that they complete a 'Where are you now?' exercise regarding their current struggles. This helps to set the groundwork for future steps on where they are going. We recommend they write down in great detail **What** their situation is now under each struggle."

"In addition, Karen and I have specific questions we suggest they consider: 1. How much time do they devote to each? 2. Which is their biggest struggle that bothers or affects them the most? 3. Is there a particular struggle that, if solved, would ease struggles in other areas as well? 4. What would it do for them, their life, or their family if they could solve this struggle? We also suggest they brainstorm ways to solve or make progress with these struggles in collaboration with fellow tribe members. After all, we're *all* in this together."

Soni paused for a moment of reflection. "I must confess that when I expressed to Rolly and Ester my frustration with the lackluster performance of most of our team, I couldn't 'get it'—why it was so poor. Yet, I now realize that I not only mismanaged them and didn't help them become *self*-managed, but also possibly overlooked the issues that many, if not most, may have been struggling with in their lives that we were unaware of. Things that potentially could have affected their performance significantly."

"That's very possible," Vicky agreed.

"I shared that we treat them fairly and with respect," Soni nodded, "And that we care for them. But not to the level that the two of you show how much you care about the women on your team. Don't get me wrong; we do care when something goes wrong in their lives. But those responses are *reactive*. What you two do is *proactive*. It's obvious. Intentional. I feel it." Soni's eyes teared as she reached out to hold Vicky and Karen's hands. "And I know the women in your tribe do, too."

"Soni. We're gonna need more tissues if you don't stop."

"I'll behave," Soni consented. "But only because I care." The three laughed.

"Thank you, Soni," Karen responded. "Part of the value and service Vicky and I provide is a yearly *'Empowering Women in Real Estate Conference.'* "

"Is that the conference you allude to in your opening message on your website?"

"It is. Each year, we select a different theme for our tribe that's relevant to current market trends or their personal lives. Some years back, Vicky came up with the theme 'Mastering the Juggle,' where we focused on how we juggle the things we struggle with in our lives."

"At these conferences, Karen and I bring in experts on each topic—guest speakers and panelists who have the experience and expertise to provide our tribe with tangible, actionable strategies that can effect real change in their lives and their business."

"You two are amazing! No wonder Ester and Rob were so pleased to learn I would be spending time with both of you."

WHERE DO I WANT TO BE AND **WHEN**?

Another thank you, Soni. As for **Where** our women want to be—where they see themselves going—goal setting is huge for us. For those who ask for our assistance, we offer help annually and strive to reevaluate them midyear. The worksheet titled **WHERE** DO I WANT TO BE AND **WHEN** should be next."

"A worthwhile goal for you *and* them," Soni replied as she turned to it.

"It is," Vicky said. "While you're at it, you might also turn to the following page with the same heading as the two go hand in hand." Soni did as Vicky suggested.

Karen shared, "As you might anticipate, for every **What** we address, a **Where** will follow, as well as a **When**. That way, they have a goal—an end in mind—to work toward. As you can see on both pages, we begin with the same five areas you saw on our STRUGGLES page."

Soni nodded, having recognized them immediately. She flipped from one page to the other. "At first glance, both look identical. What's the difference?"

"Time frame," Vicky answered, "the Fourth Key and Serving Man, **When**. On both pages, we ask that they write down where they see themselves going, **Where** they want to be in each of these areas. The first page is for the upcoming year. The second page covers a three- to five-year span."

"I like the contrasting perspectives. Short-term—more immediate. Long-term—further down the road."

WHERE – LIFE GOALS

That's the idea," Vicky confided. "In a bit, we will get to the **Real Estate Business** goals. For now, let's focus on their 'life' or 'non-production' goals, which we address on the page titled LIFE GOALS that should be next." Soni turned to that page as Vicky continued, "What good is a shelf full of production awards if you're not living a full life? When you turn eighty, we doubt you will wish you sold one more home, but rather will regret missing other experiences."

Karen added, "We want them to think about what they want for their life and identify specific goals that will support that vision. We recommend that they revisit the **WHERE** DO I WANT TO BE AND **WHEN** worksheets, perhaps setting a goal for each of those areas. As you might expect, the goals involving **Family/Relationships** mostly center around spending more quality time with loved ones."

"Rolly made me promise to spend time with my family yesterday and not research you two. I honored his request."

"Good for him, and good for you!" Karen exclaimed. "We understand he witnessed a salesperson he worked with go through a painful, costly divorce and custody battle because he was neglecting his family by spending too much time at work. Rolly vowed never to let that happen to anyone under his watch should he ever become a manager. We are told he kept that promise and still does to this day."

"That's Rolly," Soni stated.

"That's one of many reasons he, Vicky, and I mesh so well, Soni. Those goals for **Self/Health** typically involve setting aside personal time. That might mean more time for reading, meditating, hobbies, exercising, yoga, or simply getting more rest. Since **Spirituality** can be a very private matter for many, we only discuss it if they choose to share those goals."

"For **Wealth Creation/Money**," Vicky added, "some elect to put additional money they would make into savings. Others often set goals of creating a real estate portfolio by purchasing investment properties, putting their money to work for them. We offer help and advice in this area."

"These portfolios can be a gift that keeps on giving." Soni placed both hands on the one she received from Ester and Rob. "Not unlike the one I'm holding," she whispered.

WHERE AND WHY – CAST YOUR VISION

Karen whispered back, "As for their **Real Estate Business** goals, we begin by asking them to give thought to what they *truly* want from their business and **Why**. Soni, we address these on the following page titled CAST YOUR VISION."

As Soni turned to it, Vicky added, "We ask if they want to just *get by* each month, feeling bitter about how many hours they put in compared to how little they make? Or do they want to *thrive* with a growing, consistent business that builds on itself, which would mean greater ease and comfort for them?"

"Since this is not a difficult choice," Karen said, "we encourage them to record their answers from two follow-up questions: Why do they want it? And how will it positively impact their life?"

"A powerful exercise, absolutely!"

"It is, Soni. In a moment, we will discuss how we can delve much deeper into these financial goals with them. For now, we temporarily change course by discussing a topic that is seldom, if ever, discussed during goal setting. I will let Vicky begin to enlighten you with that."

WHERE – NON-NEGOTIABLES

"Thank you, Karen. Now that we're beginning to get a feel for **Where** they want to be, we address what they are not willing to give up to get there. For us, it's just as important as knowing what they want. We refer to them as 'non-negotiables.' That should be the next page you find." Soni turned to the page titled NON-NEGOTIABLES.

"As you can see, Vicky and I ask that they answer three specific questions: 1. What are they *not* willing to do or experience to reach their goals? 2. What are the things they have done or experienced that they are done with? 3. What are the things they do not want to experience again? These are quite challenging questions, and we must obtain genuine, honest answers. It's back to *'WHAT WE DO'* on our website: *'Helping women grow a successful real estate business without sacrificing their quality of life.'* "

"Karen and I are serious about this. As people, we are always saying no to something. And we must know what that no is. We don't see 'successful business' and 'quality of life' as an 'either-or' proposition. Instead, we see it as a 'both-and' opportunity."

" 'Both-and' . . . I like that," Soni remarked.

"It's more like a 'blend' as opposed to a 'balance'—a blend of both success *and* significance."

"Vicky mentioned earlier that we Virginians like wine. What we're talking about here is not unlike the art of blending a fine wine. A winemaker will tell you that blending involves a meticulous balance of key elements that define a wine's character."

"Helping the women in our tribe blend the key elements that comprise 'business success' and 'quality of life' is what helps define *their* character," Vicky suggested. "And a big component of that is knowing what does not taste good to them. For the majority of our women, the non-negotiables center around three of the struggles: **Family/Relationships**, **Self/Health**, and **Spirituality** . . . a big part of the 'life' goals we just discussed."

"Can either of you give me any examples?"

"Sure," Karen answered. "For religious reasons, they may not work on a Saturday or a Sunday, including holidays relating to their faith. Family events may also come into play. They may have a tradition of gathering with loved ones for certain holidays, and they are not willing to miss those times."

"For some," Vicky added, "conducting business on birthdays, anniversaries, or other important occasions may be a no-no. Or, they may have a 'personal day'—a day they set aside just for themselves or to give back to others. It might involve a day at the spa, a day of reading, or a day volunteering with their favorite charity or cause. It's for them to decide."

Soni responded, "All of these are their prerogative when they are self-employed. But in the corporate world, many of these may *not* be negotiable."

"True. It's all a matter of what's most important, and both we *and* they need to know that."

Karen interjected, "For safety reasons, they may not hold an open house where total strangers are at liberty to walk in."

"In the world we live in today," Soni responded, "that's understandable. That's why most builders install security cameras in their models for the safety of their people."

"Still on the topic of safety, they may not work with online or unknown leads—only referrals."

"Another non-negotiable often involves communication time," Vicky interjected. "Except for dealing with time-sensitive negotiations, they may not take calls or respond to messages before or after a certain time of day."

"I can appreciate that, too."

"Speaking of time, they may put a limit on the amount of time they're willing to devote to their business per week."

"I might need to consider doing that myself."

Karen noted, "I love the quote in **S.M.I.L.E.** from the German writer and philosopher, Goethe. 'Things which matter most must never be at the mercy of things that matter least.' " Soni nodded in agreement.

Where and **When** – Financial Goals

Since financial goals matter, let's take a look at how Vicky and I help our women discover the right blend for their financial needs. We have learned that not everyone thrives when setting big goals. Some end up feeling discouraged instead of inspired, and that defeats the purpose. That's why we offer two options from which to choose."

Vicky added, "For those who feel comfortable setting a goal they feel they can achieve—one that motivates them to go beyond where they've been without over-stressing—Karen and I suggest they complete the sheet titled GOALS FOR REALISTIC ACHIEVERS. Soni, that should be the next page in your portfolio."

As Soni turned to it, she asked, "Would this work best for the Doves and Owls of the world?"

"You know your birds from **S.M.I.L.E.**, Soni.[13] Very good! The page titled GOALS FOR BIG DREAMERS, which follows, is for the Eagles and Parrots. It's for those who are motivated by BIG goals—goals that challenge, stretch, and excite them."

As Soni turned to that page, Karen offered, "Soni, you might be interested to learn that there are more similarities than

---

[13] The ***I*** in **S.M.I.L.E.** is about IDENTIFYING the personality of the INDIVIDUAL with whom you're interacting. In place of the traditional DISC behavioral model, birds are used to represent the four styles. An Eagle represents the Dominant personality whereas the Parrot is the more talkative or Influential style. A Dove symbolizes the Steady or passive personality, and the Owl the more Compliant or analytical of the four.

differences between the two choices of goals. Since we know the differences are with the size of the goals, let's look at the similarities. Traditional goal setting focuses on achieving what one does *not* have. And yes, that's important because it represents **Where** they want to be."

"That should be a no-brainer."

"Karen and I agree, which is why we begin with just the opposite, where we actually use our brains. Our first step is to assess **What** they have, ensuring they can *keep* those things. The formula we use is simple. We begin by calculating their net income per transaction for last year. To do that, we take their average sales price and multiply it by their average commission. We then multiply that number by their commission split, which is then multiplied by the percentage they take home after taxes. That final number represents their net take-home per transaction."

"It might help to look at the example Vicky and I have given. Let's say their average sales price was $500,000, commission rate was 2.75%, commission split was 80%, and average expenses, plus taxes, accounted for another 35% (65% take-home). Multiplied out, it would look like this . . .

$500,000 x .0275 x .8 x .65 = $7,150.

That means that for each half-a-million-dollar sale, they have $7,150 of disposable income."

"Next, Karen and I look at what their bills average per month. Let's say the total is $8,000 or $96,000 for the year. If we divide that total by the $7,150, we see that they need 13.43 transactions. We would round up to 14. That equates to three-and-one-half per quarter to keep what they currently have."

"A most appropriate goal to begin with, for sure."

"Absolutely. Now that we know what numbers they need to *survive*, let's look at what they need to *thrive*! To go beyond that number, a 'Realistic Achiever' might add one to one-and-a-half more transactions per quarter. This would result in an additional net income for the year of $28,600 for the one or just over $42,900 for the one-and-a-half."

Soni responded, "I would imagine that with the tools and help you provide, they should easily accomplish that."

"They do. As for our 'Big Dreamers,' they may shoot for two or three more per quarter, which would result in an additional net income for the year of just under $57,200 for the two, or slightly under $85,800 for the three."

"I'm guessing that's doable for some?" Soni asked.

"How about for most!" Karen exclaimed. "That increase is still below the 184% figure I shared, which is the *average* growth for the entire tribe. And all of this without sacrificing their quality of life. For us, there is no other way. It's the 'both-and' paradigm we discussed earlier."

"What if they're not reaching their goals?" Soni asked.

How – Business Plan Review

We will revisit their business plan to see what went wrong—the business plan that we would have meticulously laid out at the **How** Key to get them where they want to be."

"I realize our goal for my visit is to focus on the **What** and **Where** Keys. But would you mind for just a moment if we discussed this one thing regarding the **How** Key?"

"We'd be happy to," Vicky answered. "With everything we've discussed, it's obvious that creating a business plan for their business is an absolute must. Otherwise, neither we nor they know **How** we can help them get **Where** they want to be. Creating it and then reviewing it quarterly and yearly are benefits that our women clearly see. So much so, they look forward to it."

"It's most refreshing to learn this is something they *want* to participate in. We conduct reviews with our team, and to put it mildly, most are less than excited about it."

"Not to be judgmental, Soni, but their reaction likely has to do with two things: control . . . and input. Let's discuss control first. The culture of the corporate world seems to be that of *control*—again, part of why so many women in our tribe left that world to become a part of ours."

Karen responded, "Vicky and I have been told we have a culture of *caring*, which you recognized and acknowledged. Our reviews are something we *get* to do *with* them, not *have* to do *to* them. A subtle yet significant difference."

"That's obvious, and it shows."

"Back to the magic mirrors, Soni. What we're talking about is the *reason* someone is in those mirrors. If corporate dictates that a manager conduct the reviews, that's a problem. Why? Because they know they're being managed!"

"But if they come to Karen or me for help, or accept our help by giving us permission to conduct them, then *they* are *'controlling their life and claiming their rights'* to be *self*-managed. They're empowered, not encumbered. A totally different perspective, as we discussed earlier."

"A different and very simple way, as Ester put it when she and I first met, to turn a management problem into a *self*-management opportunity."

"Unfortunately, that problem of control gets carried over into the next problem of input. We've already discussed who controls the input regarding goals, time frame, standards, work hours, and tasks performed in the corporate world. It's management, right?"

"Correct."

"But who controls this input with us?" Karen quizzed.

"They do. They determine everything."

"Correct again. And how important is that?"

"I'd say Rolly's **4th Rule of Shopping**, which we learned about in **S.M.I.L.E.**, will best answer that. ***We don't argue with our own answers.***"

"That's empowerment. That's *self*-management. It's simple."

"And Karen and I simply review their answers to the PILLARS, MAINTENANCE, STRUGGLES, NON-NEGOTIABLES, and GOALS worksheets to determine what did *not* work as planned. If the goal is out of reach for the assigned period, if it is upsetting or demotivating to them, we may need to modify a few . . . at times, many . . . or sometimes all of these areas."

"Vicky and I are aware this readjustment is not appropriate for everyone, and it's also not admitting defeat. We believe that people who feel good about themselves produce good results. And we're all seeking good results."

"To be fair," Vicky added, "the same thing applies in the event we discover they have far surpassed their goals. If they *too* easily achieved them, they're likely to feel they undershot their mark, which may take some of the wind out of their sails. If *they* so choose, we will help them reset these goals accordingly so they can feel good about meeting or exceeding a greater challenge."

"Regardless of whether they're up or down, Vicky and I also spend time at each review reflecting on what their biggest challenges were, as well as their biggest successes."

"I love that you're looking for the positives. I'm curious, does your tribe of women also have team goals?"

Where – Team Goals

You bet. In the corporate world, most organizations start with the company's goal. That number is then broken down to determine the goal for each team member. We do the opposite. We help our members identify *their* goals first. We focus on *their* unique and specific goals based on *their* individual life. Then, we combine them to make our team goal. That way we're all working and pulling together for the success of all."

"That's brilliant," Soni exclaimed.

"I don't know about brilliant," Vicky admitted. "Whatever you call it, we can tell you it works. We also track, review, and share our goals as a team so team members can provide support and cheer each other on. An exercise we've done at our annual retreat begins with each member selecting a goal they want to brainstorm with the entire team. Our team then collaborates to develop ideas and strategies to help that member achieve success, which often includes different folks working together. Several small accountability groups have formed spontaneously within our team to provide more accountability and support for those who want it."

"That's interesting. They're volunteering to join you two in the *help* and *hold* mirrors."

"Unlike the corporate approach, where everything they are expected to do and achieve is dictated from above, we involve them in the plans of where they want to be from below—from the ground up. As you might imagine, that collaborative approach can be contagious."

"It's obvious what you're doing works. It's also obvious there are no more pages in your folder, which tells me we may be done with our 'official' discussion of the **What** and **Where** Keys."

"Except for a question we have saved for later, you are correct," Karen responded. "Was there something else you wanted to cover?"

The Inner Circle Program

I was hoping to learn about your Inner Circle program that I read about earlier. Do we have time to discuss it?"

Karen glanced at her watch. "The good news is, we do. The great news is, it will take very little time to do so."

"Is it that simple, Karen?"

"Far from it. It's quite extensive. However, answering your question is simple as we've already covered most of it. Everything we have shared thus far is also part of our signature Inner Circle program."

"The distinction," Vicky interjected, "lies in how all this is accessed and delivered, and to whom it's offered. Let me explain. What we have shared with you was created for our in-house Platinum Group Real Estate team, our tribe of women, our *immediate* family. And because they are right here under our roof, it gets delivered to them in person."

"But as my idea I had while taking a shower—*Empowering Women in Real Estate*—became a reality, we recognized an opportunity to expand our family, offering it to our *extended* family, our fellow Realtors throughout the U.S. and Canada. And it gets delivered to them via the Internet when they become an Inner Circle member."

"I see the distinction now," Soni remarked.

"As a member, in addition to having access to what we've already shared, they receive a 'Plan of the Week' worksheet that identifies tasks they will need to complete to stay in touch and keep up with their marketing. Also, we provide Canva templates, graphics, and text that can be easily customized and executed."

"I don't recall discussing any of this earlier. All this is also available to your tribe?"

"Absolutely. Everything offered in this program is provided to our women. Keep in mind, Soni, that we focused our earlier discussion on the **What** and **Where** Keys and their Serving Men. What I just mentioned here pertains to the **How** Key, where the tools we provide enable them to create and execute their plan."

"Plus," Karen interjected, "every Tuesday morning, a 'Weekly Quick Lesson' video will be posted to our private Facebook Group. These bite-sized lessons go a level deeper into the program, helping them identify what they need to focus on to keep moving their business forward."

"Each month," Vicky added, "they will have the opportunity to participate in live high-level mastermind sessions with driven, focused women in the real estate industry from all across the country. These interactive sessions are designed to leave participants inspired and energized to apply what they learn in their businesses. Additionally, each month, our members have exclusive access to our real estate team's private training sessions. These trainings are led by one of us and may feature other guest experts, all designed to keep their business current, relevant, and infused with momentum!"

Karen added, "Since all sessions are recorded, they can be accessed at any time from their membership portal."

"You two have put a little time and thought into this!"

"We're far from having it all figured out, Soni, but we're making progress. Quarterly, we conduct reviews to ensure they stay on track with their goals and business objectives. And throughout the year, we walk them through a variety of critical business builders such as building and refreshing their database, and establishing and executing their annual marketing plan and budget."

"We even provide one for them," Vicky shared. "You recognize, Soni, that the last few things we mentioned pertain to the **Who** Key and its Serving Man, where we provide the help and accountability they need."

"I do. And at some point in all this, I'm guessing you would have addressed the **Why** and **When** Keys as well?"

"Oh, yes, ma'am, we cover them all. We have to."

"FYI," Karen offered, "you can learn more about our Inner Circle program on our website."

Never a Doubt

I'll read all about it," Soni replied. "Based on what we've covered, and we've covered a lot, is there any concern that with all the services and expertise you provide—whether for immediate or extended family—these persons could become dependent on you two?"

"Not at all," Karen said without hesitation. "Here's why. The goal Vicky and I have of empowering women is crystal clear. Clear to us, and clear to them. It's communicated up front and reiterated continually."

"Karen and I are here to create *self*-managed women who are capable of controlling their lives and claiming their rights without our help. Nothing short of that is acceptable. We're in the business of *growing people*, not *grooming puppets*!"

"I'm a testament to their commitment!" echoed loudly from across the room. Soni turned to see a woman standing in the doorway of the dining room. Professionally attired, with long blonde hair and dark-rimmed glasses, she exuded the look of success.

"Your timing is perfect, Robin," Vicky responded, as their new guest ran to greet her and Karen.

After the three embraced, Karen turned to introduce Soni, who was standing with open arms, excited to meet this lady. "Soni Graves, it's our pleasure to introduce you to Robin Gebhardt, one of our biggest success stories! Vicky and I took the liberty of inviting Robin and a fellow tribe member to join us for dinner."

"Biggest success stories," Soni remarked, as she and Robin exchanged hugs. "One doesn't earn that title without a lot of dedication and hard work. Congratulations, Robin!"

"You should know, Soni," Robin respectfully stated. "I've heard it through the grapevine that Rolly refers to you in the same light," she added with a wink.

"How kind of you to acknowledge that," Soni replied, graciously accepting her compliment. "You and I can count our blessings that we've been taken under the wings—you figuratively, me literally—of those who have given us their very best." Everyone chuckled at Soni's choice of words.

"We thought you and Jackie were riding together," Vicky divulged. "Is she going to be able to join us?"

"We were, but plans changed. Jackie received an offer on one of her listings and is finalizing the negotiations. She hopes to join us for dessert at the very least. If it's okay, I'll be looking for a text to see when she'll be arriving."

"That's more than okay. And good for her. Just keep us posted. That settled, let's all take a seat, and I'll ask Karen to explain to Soni why we invited you and Jackie to join us."

A Story Worth Telling

Soni, it's one thing to quote numbers regarding success. Vicky and I want to put faces to that success by having you visit with two women who are living, breathing proof that *Empowering Women in Real Estate* works. Vicky and I will take a backseat to allow Robin to share her story."

"Karen, I first want to thank you and Vicky for inviting me. What an honor." Turning to address Soni, Robin continued, "I grew up in this area and out of college invested two decades of my life in the food and beverage industry. I began with Maggiano's—a national chain that specializes in Italian-American cuisine. From their first store in Chicago in 1991, they've grown to fifty-four locations in twenty-two states. I understand you're from Texas. I believe they have several locations there."

"I am, Robin. I know of several in the Houston area. They're one of our family's favorite places to dine."

"I'm pleased to hear that. It turns out Maggiano's is the reason I have *my* family. As my career unfolded, I was entrusted with opening five of those restaurants in three states—one in Cincinnati, where I met Chris, a visiting chef from Atlanta. They discovered that his Samoan heritage and culinary talents added richness to their food. His charm and good looks added richness to my life when he became my husband."

"How special! I met my husband, Todd, in the homebuilding industry. Like me, he was also in sales." With a wink, she added, "It turns out his charm and good looks added richness to my life."

"I love that we have that in common! Were you in the same company? And was that okay?"

"We were, and it was. You ask because?"

"Because it wasn't for us per company policy. So, we moved to Nashville, where Chris became their opening executive chef, and I became the manager for The Palm—an international chain of fine-dining steakhouses that began in New York City in 1926."

"There's one in downtown Houston. I had no idea they had been around that long. So, what was it like working for two premium-brand restaurant chains?"

"I learned to handle multiple priorities and anticipate customer needs while creating and delivering five-star experiences—all skills that would help me become a confident leader. I enjoyed both the challenges and the growth opportunities that came with it. The corporate world can be rewarding. It can also be tough, particularly when it comes to quality of life. I understand, Soni, that you're in that arena."

"I am, Robin. I'm both blessed and, at times, stressed."

"Chris and I could relate to that. We wanted to have children and raise a family. A pivotal moment in our lives occurred in 2012 when I suffered a miscarriage." Robin took a deep breath as her eyes teared. "It rocked our world."

Everyone grabbed a tissue as Soni tenderly offered one to Robin. "I'm so sorry, Robin. We're back to the trials and tribulations we discussed earlier that led to Karen founding *Empowering Women in Real Estate.* What happened next, if it's not too personal to ask?"

"We began traveling, here and abroad, went on cruises, and discovered new places. I rediscovered myself. I also discovered I wanted to return to my roots—back home to this area. Chris was most supportive, as was my family, who suggested I get into real estate. We're glad I listened to them."

"Vicky and I are glad you did, too!"

"Thank you, Karen. I got my real estate license in the summer of 2013 while pregnant with our son, Sione, who is now eleven. I hung my license that next January with a brokerage in Reston, Virginia."

"Congratulations on both! That career change was okay?"

Vicky answered on Robin's behalf. "She's too humble to tell you that she won 'Rookie of the Year'!"

"Congrats! With your background, I'm not surprised."

"It likely won't surprise you to know that I also put a lot of pressure on myself. I began struggling to grow my business while balancing my family time. It's that struggle that led me to these two and to become a member of their tribe of women. I was drawn to the culture that Karen and Vicky created, where vulnerability and trust are encouraged, and compassion and support are provided. It allows you to open up and speak freely so they can better guide you."

"I notice you said guide, not manage."

"That's because they never managed me. Two decades of being managed were enough. Karen and Vicky *empowered* me to become *self*-managed. I wanted them in my mirrors. Their systems and *self*-management concepts helped me quadruple my business while enabling me to live a rich and fulfilling life with Chris and Sione. Thanks to them, I am enjoying the best of both worlds!"

"Now that I know your story, Robin, I appreciate even more the conviction in your earlier statement. You are a testament to their commitment to empowering others. You impress me as someone who is always improving, always up for a new challenge. What's next for Robin?"

"Interesting you should ask, Soni. I'm living what's next. In addition to my real estate business, with Karen and Vicky's encouragement, I founded 'Keepin' it Real with Robin!' where I coach in the industry. Staying true to my roots, I do my best to deliver the five-star service my students deserve."

"I love it when the student becomes the teacher," Soni responded with a big smile.

"Karen and I do likewise. We love her story. And we love her! And speaking of five-star service, we invited all of you to Gadsby's to also enjoy some five-star dining. If I might suggest, let's take a few minutes to refresh. That will allow Robin to check on Jackie. I've got appetizers coming out, and I'll arrange for the staff to take our dinner and beverage orders as we each come back."

Same Song, Second Verse

As the last to return, Soni was just finishing her selections when she noticed Karen, Vicky, and Robin conversing with a fourth woman—a tall brunette with a glowing smile and the kindest eyes. When the waitress left, Vicky spoke up, "To everyone's good fortune, Jackie finished early and Karen asked me to make the introductions. Soni Graves, I'm delighted to introduce you to Jackie Deane Eul, one of our newest tribe members and most recent success stories."

As they embraced, Soni smiled broadly to everyone. "Success stories seem to be a common theme here. I relish hearing yours, Jackie! I take it congratulations are in order on the sale of your listing?"

"They are, Soni. I'm very happy for the family I helped. And thanks for asking. I've been looking forward to meeting you since I got the invitation from Karen and Vicky. I've heard it rumored that Rolly trained you?"

"Yes, ma'am, it's true. I wouldn't be where I am in my career, or my life, if not for Rolly."

"I can say the same for Karen and Vicky."

"Ditto for me," Robin chimed in.

Soni turned to address Karen and Vicky. "Is there time to visit with Jackie before dinner?"

"We can consider this our happy hour," Karen proposed.

Soni smiled, "I'm happy with that." Everyone took a seat at the dining table as drinks and appetizers were served.

"Where should I begin?" Jackie asked.

"Why not start with your love for The Tide?" Vicky suggested. "And I'm not talking about laundry detergent."

Jackie grinned. "Vicky's referring to where I went to college. Growing up here, I always wanted to attend a large school with warmer weather, and the University of Alabama met that criterion. And yes, I'm a huge fan. Roll Tide!"

"That's a quality university. What was your major?"

"Political science. After college, I worked for a brief time for a congressman on Capitol Hill, but soon realized that wasn't my calling. Through a referral, I entered the real estate industry and managed luxury high-rise condos for four years. I did well and learned a lot, but that wasn't my calling either. So, I left a comfortable salary to join a small team at a local brokerage that focused on online leads."

"I admire your courage and determination to continue searching for what you were meant to do."

"Thank you, Soni. Not to brag, but I did well. That team was great for teaching me the basics and providing a foundation to handle online leads. Fortunately, these leads provided a way to begin building my database. Unfortunately, they also became my security blanket. Even worse, over time, the quality of these leads began to deteriorate. The writing on the wall told me this way of doing business was not sustainable."

"You only had one pillar in your foundation."

Jackie turned toward Karen and Vicky. "She's been paying attention, hasn't she?"

"For a Texas girl," Karen responded with a wink, "she's been holding her own so far." Everyone grinned.

"It didn't help that the 'speed-to-lead philosophy,' as it's often called, doesn't give you a good feeling about yourself. It's a hard-sell approach that leads to a lot of rejection. Its low conversion rate reflects that reality. Nor does it provide a great quality of life. We were required to put in lots of hours to make the numbers work. Those hours became stumbling blocks when you want to get married and raise a family."

"Sounds like conditions were ripe for an empowering change," Soni remarked.

"Texan or not, you're darn good!" Jackie exclaimed. The group laughed. "I was at the same brokerage with Karen and Vicky. They had a large team, and their numbers consistently outperformed those of everyone else. They were always open about who they were and their approach to business. Almost everyone on the team was a mom, and they promoted a healthy work/life blend where people and relationships came first. And they grew their business through referrals."

"The only way to do business," Robin interjected.

"Amen! I finally swallowed my pride and talked with them. To my surprise, when I asked to join their tribe, they accepted without hesitation. When we got down to business, we spent a lot of time dissecting my business—utilizing the tools and exercises they likely revealed to you this afternoon."

Soni displayed her portfolio. "They shared a ton of valuable information with me."

"They felt it important to share with me that to reach the level of success I wanted, along with the quality of life I deserved, very little time and effort would be allocated to online leads. That meant I would need to let go of my security blanket and build on my sphere of influence and referrals."

"How did you do?"

"I felt like a toddler clutching her favorite blanket. For the first year, I had a difficult time letting go. I even tried buying leads on my own, but I couldn't stomach the investment it would take to make it worthwhile. I continued to look for any way I could get leads, aside from doing what I had agreed to do. As I look back, I felt more like an addict than a toddler."

"That's tough to admit."

"It was tough to accept. But Karen, Vicky, Robin, and the rest of the team knew **What** my situation was, **Where** I wanted to be, **Why** I wanted to be there, **When** I wanted it to happen, **How** I could get there, and **Who** would help me. They never gave up on me. They were committed to helping me and holding me accountable." Jackie triumphantly raised her arms. "And look at where I am now: Enjoying my fourth year of success with the team, exceeding my goals, and married to an incredible man who is also in the business at his dad's brokerage. And thanks to our precious Madeline Rose, Larry and I are well into our second year of parenting!"

"You went from being a toddler to having a toddler. I'm so happy for you!" Soni declared. "I love your story."

Karen stood with arms spread as if speaking for Vicky and Robin. "And we love the fact that Jackie can experience this tremendous success in her business without having to outsource childcare for little Maddie."

Let's All Celebrate

As everyone stood and applauded, Vicky cried out, "Once again, that is what *Empowering Women in Real Estate* is all about!" She raised her glass to propose a toast. "I'll start this off, and we'll work our way around the table a time or two. Here's to growing a successful real estate business!"

Karen was next. "Without sacrificing our quality of life!"

Soni beamed, "To become stronger."

Jackie continued, "To become more confident."

"To control our lives," Robin joyously added.

"Let's go another round," Vicky encouraged. "To claim our rights!"

"To empowerment!" Karen roared.

"To light a fire!" Soni exclaimed, winking at Karen and Vicky.

"To the Six Keys to *self*-management," Jackie added.

"And our Six Honest Serving Men," Robin stated.

"To dreaming in the shower . . ." Vicky snickered.

". . . about empowerment," Karen grinned big, "not about the Six Serving Men!" The room filled with laughter as their glasses clinked in unison.

Sensing it appropriate, Vicky chose to share some special news. "There's one more thing that deserves a toast. Let's raise our glasses again to celebrate Karen's book, scheduled for release this fall!" Everyone cheered and toasted in celebration.

"What's the title?" Robin excitedly asked.

Jackie shouted, "What's it about?"

Soni was next. "I'm always curious to know the why behind writing a book."

Everyone's enthusiasm and interest moved Karen. "Wow. Your responses touch me! To Robin's question. After searching far and wide for just the right name, I decided on . . . *Empowering Women in Real Estate*."

Robin threw up her arms. "Imagine that," she wryly replied. "What a surprise!" Everyone chuckled.

"When something works, you stay with it, right?" she joked. "To Jackie's question. For over ten years, I have written five to seven days per week in our *Empowering Women in Real Estate* community—from personal stories and lessons learned, to inspirational and tactical tips, and everything in between. The book will be a collection of the best of these stories."

"I can't wait to read them," Jackie stated. "It will feel like getting a history lesson."

"In a way, it is. Now, to Soni's question. As I look back on the group's growth and my own evolution as a person and business owner, it's clear that growth and change are reflected in the stories we share. They deserve to be shared."

"How insightful," Soni offered. "To Vicky's credit, growth is what happens when you're in the business of growing people instead of grooming puppets."

"Vicky's right. Growing and evolving are, and should be, a part of life. We aren't meant to be the same version always and forever. Looking back, I see that growth, that evolution. But I also see the stability and the consistency of many themes, which I know have contributed to my success, and theirs."

"You never cease to amaze me," Vicky confessed. "I feel I'm in the presence of a great sage." Concerned about how that comment might be misinterpreted, Vicky felt the need to clarify her words. "Forgive me, Karen. Sage sounds old. How about in the presence of a brilliant philosopher, a storied scholar, or a deep thinker? Is that better?"

"Much better!" Karen laughingly replied. "Something's starting to get deep in here." Everyone chuckled.

What a powerful moment of celebration Soni witnessed. She felt blessed to be a part of it. The dinner conversation that ensued proved as filling as the meal. Everything under the sun was discussed: family, pets, hobbies, special interests, travel, relationships, health, successes, and setbacks. They laughed. They cried. They hugged. And they laughed some more.

Soni discovered that Karen is a proud wife of a firefighter, Josh, and a mom to sons Ben, Ryan, and Tyler. She thought it ironic that a firefighter's wife would provide the answer to what would light a fire under her people.

She learned that Vicky was born in Beirut, Lebanon, and moved to northern Virginia when she was eight. Her sons are Alex, Brandon, and Mason.

Soni also discovered that Karen's *Empowering Women in Real Estate* following has grown to over 40,000 members nationwide. *Karen's book will do well,* she thought.

Words of Advice

As the dishes were bused, Soni asked Robin and Jackie for any words of advice—since Karen and Vicky had been successful in helping them both become *self*-managed.

Robin answered first. "Three things come to mind, Soni. My first is this: clearly set the expectation up front that your goal is to empower your people. You want them to become *self*-managed." Robin paused to look each lady directly in the eye. "This goal of *self*-management is nothing new to any of us. In reality, it's nothing more than a carryover from our personal lives. Everyone at this table has children. Do any of us want to be still raising them once they're grown? I think not. Chris and I want Sione to be able to manage his own life when he grows up, to make his own decisions. We'll always be there if and when our advice and guidance are requested. But it's his life. He must own it, just as your people must own theirs! We don't want to be babysitters for life. Managers shouldn't either."

"Powerful advice, Robin. Well said!" The others nodded.

"Thank you, Soni. My second involves permission. Let's hope the people on your team who are *not* capable of *self*-managing themselves will recognize the advantages of becoming *self*-managed and will ask you to be in their mirrors. But for those who don't, I encourage you to ask them for permission to be in them, even though you're their boss and you may not feel you have to ask."

"That may be easier said than done when you're a manager."

"You're correct, Soni. That's not what *we* do when we carry that title. We want control. We're results-oriented and used to pulling strings. But during my years of managing restaurants, I learned that the more control I gave my people, the better results we all achieved."

"I appreciate that advice as well, Robin. Without their blessing, I'm managing them. With their blessing, I've been permitted to help *them* become *self*-managed. What is your third recommendation?"

"My third is to have your people set their goals first. Again, that's what Karen and Vicky did with us. That's what I'm doing with the people I'm now coaching. That wasn't done with me when I was in hospitality. Corporate set ours."

"You seem adamant about this. Can you elaborate?"

"All the years I was managed, I would have set much higher goals than what the corporation set for me. But I didn't know if it was appropriate to question theirs or to share mine, so I didn't. They were my employers. So, I began to settle for less than I was capable of doing. I'll never do that again."

"I see the wisdom in everything you shared. Thank you so much, Robin. You are a dynamo!"

"That she is," Jackie agreed. "I have two things, Soni. My first consists of three words: Stay . . . the . . . course! Every time I strayed, they would bring me back to what worked. That's why we're in their mirrors. Stay the course."

"You wouldn't be where you are today if they hadn't, would you?"

"I would not. The second involves two words: No . . . shortcuts. As I expressed earlier, had Karen and Vicky not utilized *all* the Keys, I would not be here. *Every* Key, held by *every* Serving Man, that opens *every* door to becoming *self*-managed must be used. No . . . shortcuts!"

"I see that and promise to heed your advice."

Karen felt it appropriate to comment. "When *you* use the tools, *they* learn to use them. In good time, your image will fade from the mirrors as ours did, and only theirs will be seen. *You* are necessary to make yourself *unnecessary*."

"That's profound! Initially, one might think I'm working myself out of a job. And in a way, I am. But what I'm *really* doing is freeing myself up to go to work for someone else."

"For us," Vicky declared, "that's *true* job security. We all only have so much time. Our success with the Robins of the world frees us up to then help the Jackies."

Robin placed her hands on her hips and set her jaw firmly. "So, you're saying you two used me to get to Jackie! Is that what I'm hearing?" she teasingly responded.

"In a way, I suppose we did," Vicky answered, with a wink. Everyone smiled in agreement.

Takeaways

Now to the question that Karen and I saved for you. What are *you* taking away from today?"

"I was reflecting on that during our break, and I do have something I feel strongly about," Soni said. "Yet, I must confess two things in particular that Robin and Jackie shared, which very much moved me. I want to discuss those first, if I may."

"Please do."

"I'll begin with Robin. She reiterated what the two of you had emphasized regarding the importance of setting clear expectations up front—expectations that included the goal of empowering others to become *self*-managed. As Vicky emphasized, 'Nothing short of that is acceptable!' As I champion this 'opportunity'—as Ester put it—I will have that same goal. And the laminated definition of Empowerment will be among the *first* things I discuss with my team. It reveals **Where** I expect us to be and **Why**. I *want* them to be stronger and more confident. I *want* them to take control of their lives and claim their rights! I *want* them to be *self*-managed."

"It *should* be one of the first things you share," Karen agreed. "Empowerment is *THE* answer you were searching for that would light their fire to become *self*-managed."

"That's exactly where I'm going, Karen. Should they decline this 'opportunity' . . . if they're indifferent to it . . . or if there's no spark, no fire, I will have discovered what I needed to know. As Robin alluded to, some may not want to grow up. Should any of these clues be clear, my position on *their* position will, too. I'll be respectful. As well as direct. And I will encourage them to take their excellence elsewhere! I have no wish to be a babysitter. I'm resigning my role as puppet master!" Everyone loudly applauded Soni's message.

"That obviously struck a nerve," Robin acknowledged. "I almost didn't go there at the risk of offending anyone."

"I'm grateful you did, Robin. I want a team of grown-ups who *are* grown up."

Soni turned to address Jackie. "Your advice to 'stay the course' also got my attention. If they invite or allow us to be in their mirrors, our commitment to providing the help they need and holding them accountable can never waver. NEVER! Unless they die, or quit, we're sticking with it!" Again, everyone applauded.

"You *and* they will be thankful you did," Jackie revealed.

"Karen and I can appreciate why these resonated with you. And we respect and agree with your position on both. Now, what is your takeaway that you feel strongly about?"

Soni paused and gently smiled. "Love—I know it's not the most professional business-like image, I'm sorry. It's love. I now firmly believe that love should be at the heart of everything we do. Based on what I've read, seen, heard, and felt these past hours, the two of you have done a masterful job of creating a *culture* of love." Soni's answer touched everyone. "Karen, without question, you and Vicky love what you do. You love the business you're in. You love your tribe of women. And I love the way they have responded to that love."

Vicky smiled. "We told you Virginia was for lovers!"

"Texas might be, too—at least this one. I love what I do. I love our business. And I love our team."

"Everything we've seen, heard, and felt from you validates your words."

"Thank you. I also love my company. It's been good to me. For that matter, it's been good to a lot of people. We do many things right. That makes me proud. We could do many things better. That gives me hope. I hope we don't become complacent, content with staying where we are."

"No person, no team, no organization ever got better by marching in place," Karen affirmed. "We must always be moving forward, willing to step outside our comfort zone. Whether it's a person, a team, or an organization, to get better, we must learn to be comfortable being uncomfortable."

Soni repeated her words, "Be comfortable being uncomfortable. An interesting way of looking at growth and change."

Robin spoke up, "I feel compelled to share something. I've heard *love*, *heart*, and *team* mentioned—words found in a quote I use in my coaching, which I believe each of you will appreciate. Who is familiar with the name Vince Lombardi?"

Jackie's arm shot up like a young schoolgirl. "I am, Robin! The Lombardi Trophy is awarded to the winner of the Super Bowl. It's named after him. Nick Saban, our coach at Alabama, would often reference a quote Mr. Lombardi is famous for. 'Winning isn't everything; it's the *only* thing!' "

"Excellent, Jackie. You know your football and your quotes. And that *is* the one he is most known for. But there's another, less famous quote that revealed his *secret* to winning, perhaps one that required him to be comfortable being uncomfortable. 'I don't necessarily have to like my players,' he said, 'but as a man, I must *love* them. *Love* is loyalty. *Love* is teamwork. *Love* respects the dignity of the individual. Heart power is the strength of your team.' "

"*That's* the quote he *should* be known for," Vicky exclaimed. "It's obvious he believed in a culture of love."

Soni nodded. "I agree. To hear 'love' being referenced from a very tough man in what is considered a very tough sport says a lot about its power. Thank you for sharing that, Robin."

Soni turned to address Karen and Vicky. "Vince Lombardi built a winning team with a culture of love. You two have done the same. I'm determined to do likewise. I'm hopeful that the success of our team will inspire other divisions to follow our lead, and that our accomplishments will have a positive impact on them. For that matter, I'd love to see other companies do the same. Our industry would benefit immensely if that were to happen. I'm hopeful love will get us there."

"If I may, I have a quote to offer that might be pertinent to our discussion," Jackie stated as she glanced at Karen. "A mentor of mine once told me that 'Love is the bridge between you . . . and *everything*!' "

Karen smiled. "I'm touched you remembered. That's a quote from the Persian poet and scholar Rumi, which dates back to the twelfth century. To empower someone *is* to love them. In the business world, empowering others to become *self*-managed is the ultimate expression of love. Love is the bridge that got all of us where we needed to be."

Simple . . . But Not Easy

Speaking of getting where one needs to be," Robin stated, "Jackie and I need to get home to tuck some kiddos in for the night." Jackie gave Robin a thumbs-up.

"Karen and I have a houseful of boys to check on as well."

"And I have family I need to call before I call it a night," Soni chimed in. "Rolly also asked that we check in each evening to debrief. He has booked me on a morning flight to San Antonio to meet with some folks after lunch who will address the **Why** and **When** Keys to *self*-management."

"Cheri and Craig, right?" Karen asked.

"Yes, ma'am. How did you know?"

"We were on a Zoom call with them this morning, as well as Ester and Rob. It also included Hal, Rick, and Tiffany, who you'll be meeting with on Thursday afternoon. We all wanted to get up to speed on who would be covering what."

Vicky added, "You will be excited about the tools that all of them will be sharing. We will begin integrating them as well into what we do for our women."

Soni smiled. "I've got a lot to look forward to."

"That you do!" Karen exclaimed. "Since Vicky and I drove together, we insist on dropping you off where you're staying."

"Thank you. I'll gladly accept the offer. Will you all allow me to offer to pay for tonight's dinner?"

"Not gonna happen. Rolly took care of that when he reserved this room. You're a day late and a dollar short."

"The story of my life!" Soni remarked with a smile. "Rolly is always so thoughtful and generous, just as all of you have been with your wisdom and time."

On that note, Robin and Jackie hugged everyone and said goodbye. Karen and Vicky walked them to the door. Returning, they found Soni fixated on the image of the ***Self-*** **Management Model**. Vicky said, "Once again, we find you immersed in your thoughts. Is it time for another selfie?"

"Oh, my! Please forgive me *again*. I'm just amazed at how simple this is. I can't wait to begin applying it with my team."

"We know the feeling," Karen responded. She received a nod of approval from Vicky. "It *is* simple, but it's *not* easy. You realize it will take a lot of effort on your part to make it happen."

"I do," Soni agreed. "And I will draw inspiration to stay the course from the message from your website . . .

Helping women grow a successful real estate business without sacrificing their quality of life.

I cannot wait to do the same for my team—for my ladies *and* my gentlemen—for all my managers *and* all their people," she added with a smile that lit up the room.

"We're flattered," Vicky stated. "Just remember, it all goes back to Rolly's second requirement of Sherri—it's all about accountability, for you *and* them. When I get home tonight, I'll email you the files of everything we provided, including those you received from Ester and Rob."

Karen added, "Cheri and Craig agreed to do the same after tomorrow's visit, as did Hal, Rick, and Tiffany following your meeting with them Thursday. This will allow you to have clean originals for your managers and all their people."

"Thanks for the reminders, from both of you, and for everything you shared. And thanks again for the gifts. You two are the best!" The three embraced for what seemed an eternity. A forever bond had been forged for which all three were grateful.

As they made their way down the steps of Gadsby's Tavern and onto the softly lit streets of Old Alexandria, Soni pictured how John and Abigail Adams and the Founding Fathers must have felt when they took these same steps. She imagined they were excited about pursuing the goal of an entire nation becoming *self*-managed. They must have known what they were about to embark on would not be easy, but they were determined to make it happen. Two hundred and fifty years later, Soni knew she was excited about pursuing the goal of an entire organization becoming *self*-managed. It might not be easy either, but she was determined to make it happen.

Section 5:
WHY AND WHEN

Opportunities Abound

Upon exiting the security checkpoint at the San Antonio airport, Soni spotted a striking woman seated at a café table. *She exactly matches the description Rolly gave me!* "You must be Cheri Bass," she confidently declared, approaching the lady.

"That would be me," Cheri cheerfully responded as she stood to hug Soni. "And you must be Soni Graves."

Soni smiled wide. "That would be me. Rolly was right when he said to look for a younger version of Christie Brinkley. Are you ever mistaken for her?"

Cheri blushed. "Quite often, I'm embarrassed to say. You also were easy to recognize. Rolly said I could spot your radiant smile a mile away. The 'Virginia is for Lovers' ball cap and T-shirt he said you'd be wearing were a giveaway, too."

Soni sported an even bigger smile. "I guess so, Cheri. Thanks to Rolly and some folks he's introduced me to, I have a lot to smile about. Next week, I have the opportunity to begin empowering my team to become *self*-managed. I cannot wait."

"We both have a lot to smile about. Thanks to our feathered friend and some folks he's introduced me to, beginning next week, I *also* have the opportunity to help a sales team right here in San Antonio become *self*-managed. And *I* can't wait."

"How exciting!" Soni exclaimed. "It seems opportunities abound for both of us." Cheri's revelation sparked Soni's curiosity. "At some point, Cheri, is there time for you to tell me how this came about?"

Cheri checked her watch. "Considering the purpose of your visit, it would be most appropriate. And since your flight arrived early, we have time now. Why don't we take a seat? I can finish my coffee, and the iced tea is for you—compliments of Ester and Rob. Oh, before I forget, have you had lunch?"

"Yes, ma'am, during my layover in Dallas. Thanks for asking." Soni placed her carry-on and handbag under the table and took a seat. "How thoughtful of Ester and Rob. I take it you learned about that from your call with everyone yesterday."

"I did, Soni. I also learned you ask great questions and are a terrific listener."

"Thank you. I've got a lot to learn. On my flights today, I got busy reviewing the materials everyone gave me and began organizing my thoughts about how I will apply them. Speaking of being busy, I must thank you for your willingness to pick me up. I hope it wasn't too much of an inconvenience. Rolly said you insisted."

"It's my pleasure. And, my presence at the airport now is related to my new opportunity. I just dropped off my husband for a flight to Orlando. Jerrell will drive back this weekend with our two golden retrievers, along with the rest of our belongings. We just moved here last week. The timing worked to stay here and pick you up."

"Congratulations! May I ask what prompted the change?"

"Not at all. Fourteen months ago, we were struggling."

"I'm sorry to hear that. Surely it wasn't career-wise?"

"No, ma'am. Quality-of-life-wise."

"Your response is timely considering the enlightening discussion regarding 'struggles' I had with Karen and Vicky."

"Which I also had with them on our call. You see, Jerrell and I were both enjoying successful careers with national builders in the Orlando market. He, in sales. I, in sales management. We were dedicated to our profession and kept our noses to the grindstone. It's possible our inability to have children contributed to our work consuming us. Looking back, I guess we simply weren't happy. 'Burned out' might be a better way to describe it. We struggled to balance work and play."

"It can happen, Cheri. So, what did you do?"

"Since we were in good health, and thankfully still are, we realized we weren't getting any younger. We also knew we loved to travel. So, we sold our home, bought a large motorcoach that could tow our vehicle, loaded up Chase and Clancy, and traveled the country. An amazing experience."

Soni reached for her handbag to retrieve her portfolio. "Good for both of you. And Chase and Clancy," she added with a grin. "I admire your courage." She quickly flipped to the STRUGGLES page and pointed to the questions Karen and Vicky would pose to the women in their tribe. "I have to ask you about these," she stated as she read them aloud. "*1. How much time do they devote to each? 2. Which is their biggest struggle that bothers or affects them the most? 3. Is there a particular struggle that, if solved, would ease struggles in other areas as well? 4. What would it do for them, their life, or their family if they could solve this struggle?* Correct me if I'm wrong, Cheri, but if you and Jerrell had managers who had proactively addressed these questions—assuming you did not—is it possible the two of you might have made a different decision?"

"Fair question, Soni. Who knows? I'm confident it wouldn't have hurt. At least we would have felt they cared."

"We're constantly presented with life lessons, Cheri. Did you learn anything from this that will help you with empowering your new team to become *self*-managed?"

"Without question. Along with getting to know them as people, I *must* know what they're struggling with. And just as important, I've got to help them maintain a healthy 'blend' of success *and* quality of life as Karen and Vicky have so masterfully done with their tribe of women. I've always known that both production and the ability to produce are important. Karen and Vicky helped me recognize I must focus on the health of the goose first—the eggs second."

"I came to the same conclusion after my time with those two. So, how did you end up here?"

"All play wasn't working either. We missed people. I missed growing a team. Rolly knew this and also knew of a private builder in San Antonio who was searching for a VP of sales. He made the introduction. I start full-time next week."

"Congrats! Are your new company and team excited?"

"Yes, ma'am. And yes, ma'am. Both are expecting me to do what I did during the years I grew my team in Orlando."

"Would you mind sharing what those accomplishments were, and what their expectations might be?"

"Gladly, Soni. By helping my team learn how to create a homebuying experience built on relationships, our sales more than doubled in just five years. My new company would like its sales to grow, too."

"Who wouldn't?"

"By focusing on the quality of those relationships, we were able to cut our cancellation rate almost in half."

"It works every time."

"It does. In addition, Soni, we increased our JD Power customer satisfaction rating by twenty-three percent, which resulted in more referrals."

"They go hand in hand."

"Yes, they do. Oh, and before I forget, our division made more money, a *lot* more money."

"Funny how that happens."

"It is, isn't it? As a result, we became the company's number one team in the nation."

"Most impressive, Cheri."

"Thank you, Soni. Best of all, I ended up with a team of *self*-managed individuals. And that is what everyone at my new opportunity is *most* excited about."

"I don't blame them. You say you *ended up* with a *self*-managed team. That wasn't by design?"

"It was, but it wasn't. Let me explain. My mom was a CPA, very left-brained, very logical. Dealing with the financial aspect of her clients' portfolios, she understood the importance of business plans. Since it all made sense, or 'added up' as she would say, she brought that mindset into how our family functioned. We actually made a *family* business plan each and every year."

"That's most interesting, Cheri. Did that influence you when you entered the workplace?"

"Absolutely. I mean, how can you get where you want to be without goals and a plan of how to get there? After I graduated college, I eventually got into homebuilding with a small builder. Since they had no sales manager, I created my own business plan. *I* was responsible for my success. To me, it just made sense. It also 'added up' financially. Not to brag, but I was always their top salesperson."

"To be expected! You know, I can't name one salesperson who has *ever* created a business plan on their own."

"Nor can I. As Rolly might say, I was a strange bird. When I went to work for a national builder, I brought that paradigm with me and was consistently a top-producer. When I moved into management, I expected my salespeople to do the same—to create *their* business plan. That meant they set their own goals and specified *how* they would make that happen. Just like Karen and Vicky, I had to help my tribe. But together, we got there. By the way, they always exceeded the company's goals. To me, *they* needed to be responsible for their success, which one could interpret as being *self*-managed. *I* was successful because *they* were successful."

"Thanks for sharing that with me. I'm all for that. And I know my people will be, too."

Cheri glanced at her watch. "I'm all for us being on time for our meeting. Let's gather our stuff and head to where I'm parked. Craig is anxious to meet us both."

"So, you haven't met him yet?" Soni inquired as they gathered their belongings and headed toward the parking lot.

"Not in person. As you know, building relationships with the local real estate community is a top priority for homebuilders, so my assistant scheduled me to meet with him next week. Rolly's call this weekend changed all that."

"My apologies, Cheri. I feel selfish that everyone has adjusted their schedules based on my needs."

"Soni, none of us took it that way. When Rolly explained you were concerned about your people, and that the situation was quite urgent, we were excited to help someone that excited about helping others." With a subtle wink, Cheri continued, "Candidly, this allowed me to begin building a relationship with the owner of the largest Keller Williams franchise in the U.S. a whole week sooner. I should be thanking *you*."

Soni smiled. "In that case, I'm glad I could be of help."

On the drive to Craig's office, the two enjoyed an upbeat conversation, discovering many things they had in common: both grew up in small towns—Soni in West Texas, Cheri in North Florida; both had sales experience in pharmaceuticals before new home sales; each met their husband in new home sales; oh, and they both loved people and this business.

A Sign of Things to Come

As Cheri pulled into the KW Heritage parking lot, she was excited to find a covered spot that offered shade from the summer heat. They both laughed when they noticed the sign on the post just in front of their space. ***Life's short. Smile while you still have teeth***.

"How cute," Cheri remarked. As they grabbed their handbags and walked along the covered spaces, they noticed another. ***Behind every successful person, there is a substantial amount of coffee***. And then another. ***I'm not a magician, but I can turn For Sale into Sold!*** There must have been a dozen or more.

Soni pointed to one she liked. "This has to be my favorite: ***Whatever you do, always give 100%, unless you're giving blood.*** I love the humor in these. I'm anxious to discover the source and the story behind them." Cheri nodded. The two made their way to the front of the building, impressed by its size and setting—three stories surrounded by majestic live oaks. "If this was built with the intent to make a statement for agents, buyers, and sellers," Soni added, "mission accomplished."

The wow factor continued in the lobby. A soaring twenty-two-foot ceiling, marble floors, plush sofa and chairs, a coffee bar with hot cocoa, a Starbucks machine, a mini-fridge, an assortment of drinks and snacks, and a gigantic eight-by-twelve-foot monitor displaying KW Heritage listings.

A lady behind the reception desk stated, "You must be Craig's guests. He'll be right out. Can I offer either of you a refreshment?"

"That's us," Cheri smiled. "And yes, ma'am, I'll take a water, please. Thank you."

"Do you happen to have an unsweetened tea?" Soni asked as the receptionist handed Cheri a water.

"She doesn't," a man shouted as he approached from the hallway, "but I do." Soni looked up to find a handsome, stocky gentleman with broad shoulders and a shaven head standing before them. "I understand this is your drink," he stated as he handed Soni a bottle of unsweetened tea. "I'm Craig Owen, and you must be Soni Graves. I can offer you a handshake, but I'm known for giving the best hugs in San Antonio. I'm okay either way. Out of respect, I always ask."

Soni smiled. "Well, I'm just gonna have to try one of those *best* hugs," she responded as they embraced. "It's a pleasure to meet you, sir. And by the way, that was a great one. Oh, and thanks for the tea," she added with an even bigger smile.

"You're welcome, Soni." He turned to address Cheri. "I recognize you from yesterday's Zoom call, Cheri. I must say, you're even lovelier in person. Handshake or hug?"

Cheri blushed. "I prefer one of those *best* hugs, too," she answered as the two embraced. "And thank you, sir, for the compliment. And *I* must say you are even more distinguished in person."

"Well, thank you, ma'am," Craig responded as he pretended to run his fingers through hair he didn't have. "It would appear you and I are both members of 'The Mutual Admiration Society.' " Laughing as he turned to Soni, he asked, "Would you care to join our little club?"

Soni grinned. "I'd be honored, thanks. You remind me of Mr. Clean—in a good way." Craig smiled. "Should Cheri and I call you Mr. Owen, or would you prefer Craig?"

"I've been compared to Mr. Clean more than once, Soni, and take it as a compliment. As for Mr. Owen or Craig, I prefer to be called in the Caribbean, but that won't be happening today," he playfully answered. "Craig will be just fine."

"Craig it is," Soni responded. "I appreciate your sense of humor. Did you have anything to do with the signs in the parking lot? I'm guessing there's a story there."

"Several stories, to be candid. One of our senior agents suggested we install reserved parking signs for our veterans. With four military bases in our market, we have a significant number of veterans serving as agents and many more as customers. Their reserved signs are to show our respect and appreciation for their sacrifice and service to our country."

Cheri interjected, "That has to make them feel good."

"It makes all of us feel good as they always thank us when they come inside. After installing them, another of our agents suggested we create reserved spots for expectant moms. We listened. These women also respond favorably. All those reserved spots are to the left of where you came in."

"We didn't notice those, but we're glad you mentioned them. We were asking about those under the covered parking."

Craig sheepishly bowed his head like a little boy. "*Wel-l-l* . . . I may have to take a *lit-t-t-tle* credit for those. We derived such pleasure from the first signs, we decided to take it to another level, which is why the ones you and Soni referenced came about. I *have* to have fun at what I do, and I want it to show in everything *we* do. It's the ***E*** philosophy in **S.M.I.L.E.** I tell my agents, 'Don't take life so seriously; we're not gonna get out of it alive anyway!' " Both ladies laughed.

"You are impressive," Soni stated, "as is this building. Any chance we could get a tour while we're here?"

"I'd be honored. But *after* Cheri and I focus on why you're here. Let's step over to our meeting room for a little privacy."

They followed Craig down the hall until he stopped to open a set of double doors. They entered a massive room filled with tables and chairs. TV monitors graced every wall, with a large grease board in the front and a wooden podium with sound equipment off to the side. Craig suggested they take a seat at a smaller table, which held a folder, an assortment of colored markers, and a box of tissues.

Soni scanned the room. "Wow, you must be able to seat several hundred people in here. This is enormous!"

"Accurate guess, Soni," Craig answered. "With no tables, we can accommodate around one-third of our twelve hundred agents. In addition to training and meetings, we offer it for community events and nonprofit organizations to gather."

"That's a lot of room and a lot of agents," Soni exclaimed.

Cheri spoke up, "Please forgive me. I know this afternoon is not about me, but if only a fourth of them sold just one new home with my builder, that would meet our business plan for the entire year."

"This afternoon can be about you, too, Cheri," Craig stated. "Our meeting next week would have been about how our companies could help each other grow. Your company builds an excellent home and has a stellar reputation. We already bring a lot of buyers your way. That said, we have a ton of new agents who likely don't even know you or your builder exists." Craig softly whispered, "It's a shame we don't know someone who could help remedy that situation."

Soni pointed to Cheri as she whispered, "This lady may be just what the doctor ordered." Everyone smiled.

A Matter of Worth

I think you're on to something, Soni. Speaking of new people, just last night, one of our newest agents, a nineteen-year-old, Sam Adams, who was referred to us by Rolly, hosted a networking event for young entrepreneurs in this portion of the room." Craig pointed to the rear wall. "Folding panels allow us to divide it into smaller areas for a more intimate setting. For this event, Sam created a professional brochure, sent out invitations, catered a meal, and invited two speakers to share their expertise and advice. I understand that more than fifty young men and women attended. It was a nice turnout."

"Good for him. As he's new, I'm impressed he thought of something that creative and was able to pull it off."

"Not bragging, but that's expected when you attract the right people, expose them to great training, provide them with the tools they need, offer help and guidance, and empower them to take ownership of their business. For us, it's about *worth*—the '*worth*while work' Ken Blanchard writes about in his book, *Gung Ho!* Our KW Mission promotes worth:

To Build CAREERS *worth* having,
BUSINESSES *worth* owning,
LIVES *worth* living,
EXPERIENCES *worth* giving, and
LEGACIES *worth* leaving.

"Which all leads to *self*-worth," Cheri stated. "So, you met Sam through Rolly. I'm curious how you and Rolly met."

"From another referral, Mr. James Smothers. Yes, *the* James Smothers in the ***M*** in **S.M.I.L.E.**"

"I loved his story. As I recall from the book, he lives in San Antonio. I would love to meet him one day."

Craig winked and whispered again, "I might know someone who could make that happen."

Soni responded, "I bet you do." She turned to address Cheri. "I meant to ask earlier how you and Rolly met."

"Like you, I was one of his students. We've stayed in touch over the years, and Jerrel and I actually stayed in our motorcoach on his property during our sabbatical. I was fortunate that when he learned of the opening in San Antonio, he immediately reached out to me. And when he contacted me this weekend about your 'opportunity,' *I* jumped at the opportunity to meet you and be of help."

"I'm grateful you did."

"What comes around, goes around. I confess, with the new tools I discovered on our Zoom call yesterday, I'm confident I can help my new team become *self*-managed—in a much easier, time-saving way."

Soni reached under the table to pull out her portfolio. "I've got an empty tab just waiting for more new tools and ideas you and Craig can share. Who's going to start?"

Filling in the Gaps

Craig responded, "Since I've got home court, I'll do the honors. First, Soni, before we address the **Why** and **When** Keys, it's essential to note that Karen and Vicky have already covered most of what Cheri and I were prepared to cover. So, we'll be filling in the 'gaps' with a few additions. That means our visit may be notably shorter than theirs was yesterday."

Cheri smiled. "Which means we can get you checked into your hotel sooner and get an earlier start on our evening on the San Antonio River Walk. I've never been there and am so looking forward to it."

"I understand that's where I'm staying," Soni replied, "and oh, Cheri, you're gonna love it. It's the heart of the city, combining the natural beauty of the river with some of the best dining, entertainment, and shopping anywhere."

"Shopping," Cheri flashed her signature smile. "Did I hear shopping?"

Craig grinned. "Okay, ladies. Simmer down. We need to focus on why we're here." They both grinned. "After the others signed off the call yesterday, Cheri and I identified several areas we believe will be most helpful."

Cheri added, "And since Karen and Vicky effectively covered the **When** Key and its Serving Man, Craig and I will focus our attention on the **Why** Key."

Craig interjected, "I've printed and three-hole punched the documents we will be discussing. I can hand them to you one by one or all at once. Your choice."

"Thanks for asking and for printing them. Let me put them all in, and we'll see how that works," Soni replied as she inserted the documents behind the tab she had labeled 'San Antonio Visit.' "

"Before we get to the materials, let's talk about perspective. At KW, we view ourselves as a technology company that provides *the* real estate platform our agents, buyers, and sellers prefer. We think like a top producer, act like a trainer-consultant, and focus all our activities on service productivity and profitability. You and Cheri can learn more about this and all I'll be discussing by visiting our website."

"I expect Cheri and I will do just that. Thanks."

"At KW University, we offer twelve Core Power Sessions along with twenty-three Exclusive Courses. Our beginning course for new agents is titled IGNITE—Skills to Spark a Great Career."

"I find it interesting, Craig, that the title reflects the answer I was searching for as to what would light a fire under my people to want to become *self*-managed."

"You will discover many similarities. We understand that Ester and Rob, as well as Karen and Vicky, frequently discussed perspectives. The very first learning experience for our new agents pertains to SIX PERSONAL PERSPECTIVES. That should be the top page." Soni nodded as she brushed her hand over it.

SIX PERSONAL PERSPECTIVES

Craig continued, "As you can see, the first involves committing to 'Self-Mastery.' They need to know their goals, their strengths and weaknesses, and how to work with both to master the necessary knowledge, skills, and habits to reach their goals."

Cheri interjected, "Yet another way to describe *self-management.*"

"Exactly," Craig acknowledged. "The second is also about commitment—committing to the 80/20 Principle. It's the realization that twenty percent of all their actions lead to eighty percent of all their results."

Soni stated, "Obviously, the key is to identify what that twenty percent is and focus on it."

"Amen. The third is to move from an 'Entrepreneurial Approach'—doing what comes naturally . . . to a 'Purposeful Approach'—doing what comes *un*naturally."

Soni remarked, "Karen said we have to be comfortable being uncomfortable. That's the only way growth occurs. Or as Ester and Rob might say, no pain–no gain!"

"True," Craig agreed. "The fourth is to make being 'Learning-Based' the foundation of your action plan."

Cheri added, "I encouraged my team to read books, listen to podcasts, and learn from others. It's about constant improvement. There's always a better way to do everything."

Soni interjected, "The first requirement Rolly had for Sherri—to be willing to learn."

"You're right," Craig confirmed. "The fifth is to replace 'Limiting-Beliefs' with '*Un*limiting-Beliefs.' "

"Limiting beliefs can be paralyzing," Soni confessed. "If you believe you can't, you won't. It's that simple."

"Yes, it is, Soni," Craig confirmed. "I'm confident you and Cheri will appreciate the last one: be accountable."

Soni wiggled her fingers. "The last requirement Rolly had for Sherri—to hold herself ac*COUNT*able."

"The **Who** key," Cheri added.

"Right on both accounts, ladies. The next document, titled FOUR LAWS OF A DATABASE, pertains to the discussion of Pillars and Maintenance you had with Karen and Vicky." Soni turned to that page.

WHAT – FOUR LAWS OF A DATABASE

During our conversation yesterday," Craig continued, "Vicky mentioned Pillars represented sources of leads—where their business comes from for both listings and sales. We refer to it as their 'Sphere of Influence,' or SOI. We identify fourteen sources or categories. Regardless of how many they have, this document reminds them of four laws they need to follow with that database of individuals to build a successful career."

Soni stated, "I see the first is to *build* a database and the second is to *feed it* every day. Both make sense."

"They do," Craig agreed. "For their business to grow, *it* must grow. That's precisely what Sam Adams was doing last night—growing his database. And what's next for the 'Sams' of the world is specified in the last two laws: Use it to *communicate* with those in their database systematically. And *service* all leads."

Cheri spoke up, "From what we discussed with Karen and Vicky, they did a great job of emphasizing the importance of the cards, calls, text messages, personal visits, email newsletters, and events necessary to maintain it."

Craig added, "That they did. I like the message from our founder, Gary Keller. In his book, *The Millionaire Real Estate Agent*, he states, 'To succeed at a high level in real estate sales, you must commit to frequent contact with a database with the intent of building close relationships.' "

Soni interjected, "So true, Craig. If I might add, it's the secret behind the phenomenal success John Norris experienced. 'I'm not a great salesperson,' he said. 'What I am is a great *relationship* person.' It's about the people you develop great relationships with. You stay in touch with them. You add value to their lives. And you ask them to help you help others."

"To me," Craig added, "it's an unselfish act of love and kindness. You care about others, and you put their needs and interests first."

"It is *all* about love and kindness, Craig," Soni said. Cheri nodded in agreement.

"Soni, the next document to discuss is titled CHOOSE AN ACCOUNTABILITY PARTNER." Soni flipped to that page.

WHO – CHOOSE AN ACCOUNTABILITY PARTNER

This document is divided into three parts: Guidelines, Choosing a Partner, and Questions," Craig began. "Let's begin with the Accountability Guidelines part: Provide a safe place to share. Follow through with action items. Listen attentively while the other person shares. Set a frequency of checking in with each other. Dig deep to find out why you do the things you do. Respect each other and the process. Create a commitment and stick to it. Be open to receiving feedback. Give specific feedback. Have each other's best interests in mind."

"This is most helpful, Craig. It pertains to the **Who** Key and Serving Man. I like the fact that everything is spelled out in black and white. It reduces the risk of misunderstandings."

"It does, Soni. Choosing a Partner delves into more specifics: the Accountability Partner's Name, Contact Information, and Goals, as well as the Frequency of Accountability Check-Ins; Date, Time, and Location of the First Check-In are also specified."

"So, what are the Accountability Questions about?"

"They open up opportunities for productive discussion: 1. How did you do? 2. How do you feel about that? 3. Did you have any opportunities for improvement? 4. How will you address those opportunities? 5. What were your wins? 6. How will you celebrate your wins?"

"Very thorough, Craig. It appears these will apply to the mirrors on either or both walls behind the doors opened by the **Who** Key."

Cheri spoke up, "That's precisely what they do, Soni. From the perspective of an outsider looking in, it's as if this entire accountability piece was written with the **Who** Key and the mirrors in mind."

"It does," Craig responded. "It's interesting how closely the philosophies mesh. I suppose great minds *do* think alike."

Soni responded, "It's refreshing, for sure."

"Perhaps the most profound of those commonalities involves the **Why** Key that relates to the YOUR BIG LIFE portion of our IGNITE training. It should be the next page." Soni turned to it.

WHY – YOUR BIG LIFE . . . YOUR BIG WHY

Soni spoke up, "The image of the eight blank boxes arranged like the hours on a clock connected by dotted lines to the blank circle in the middle has certainly caught my attention."

"It does most," Craig answered. "The blank boxes are where you enter the things important in your life."

Soni politely interrupted, "Such as family, relationships, our business, ourselves, our health, our spirituality, and our wealth—the struggles Karen and Vicky mentioned."

"Exactly, Soni. Things important to you. Goals can come into play here, too. Money for travel, a second home, a sports car, a boat, or a college fund for kids might show up."

"And can I assume *you* are in the center of all these?"

"Yes, ma'am, *you* are at the center—the center of the things that give you your **Why**—or in KW terms, Your Big Why. As Gary Keller sees it, 'Your Big Life leads you to Your

Big Why.' It's about having a purpose, a mission, or a need that, in turn, gives you focus. To again quote from his book, 'To achieve success, you need motivation and inspiration for doing it—Your Big Why.' "

Cheri spoke up, "Getting to **Why** is what helped me land and keep one of my most successful salespeople. When I first met Craig McCaskill, he was selling timeshares in Orlando. Along with the others on that team, he was provided a comfortable salary but low commissions. Even though he was in that team's top five, his income potential was limited. That income didn't match the lifestyle Craig desired—a nice car, a plush home, money to take a date on an amazing dinner, funds to travel, money for golf."

Soni grinned, "I think Craig's clone is on my team."

Craig chimed in, "He's on a lot of teams. What a coincidence that Craig and I share the same name. I can relate to him in my younger years."

"I'll bet we all can," Cheri confessed. "But there was another thing about selling timeshares that was not a match for Craig and was every bit as important as all this—his values. He truly cared about people. He wanted to know about the people *as* people. He wanted to build a relationship. Selling timeshares is about closing, not caring. Salesmanship, not relationships. I offered a solution for income *and* outcome."

Soni quizzed, "He not only came on board, but he was also extremely successful, wasn't he?"

Cheri smiled. "He did, he was, and he is. And he has been invited to visit San Antonio. I'll give you three guesses as to who extended that invitation, and the first two don't count!"

Craig smiled. "I take it you're talking about a home with you and not KW Heritage?"

"I'm for whatever works best for Craig," Cheri answered, "as long as it's me!" Everyone grinned.

Life in the Key of **Why**

I'd like to share a personal story regarding the significance of **Why** that not many people know about," Craig stated. Both ladies scooted their chairs closer to the table. "**Why** is my favorite of the Six Keys. Here's why. I was adopted as a newborn, as was my older brother. Our adoptive parents deeply loved us, and I thank God every day for them. They are the reason for my success. Their emotional bank account was overflowing. Their financial bank account was not. They wanted the best for us, but they were limited in what they could provide; may their souls rest in peace. Their financial woes contributed to their divorce when I was twelve. It was heartbreaking to watch." Both ladies reached for tissues. "My Big Why—what drives me to be successful—is not about me and what I can get. It's about others and what I can give. I wanted my kids to have a better life than my parents were able to provide for my brother and me. That's why I've busted my tail to make certain that happened. My Big Why is about my five kids and what I can give to them."

Soni spoke up, "Thanks for sharing that, Craig. I feel that passion, that conviction in your voice. If Cheri and I were to see that completed image of YOUR BIG LIFE, I expect we would notice two differences. First, the circle would be a heart.

Second, your kids would be in the middle of that heart *with* you." Cheri nodded in agreement.

Craig grasped each by the hand and gave a gentle squeeze. "Aw, thank you. I appreciate you saying that. Now that I think about it, my extended family—all of my KW Heritage agents—would be in there, too!"

Cheri remarked, "You realize that makes for one ginormous circle, don't you?"

"I do. And interesting enough, there's room for that circle to grow. My Big Why is about others. The more the merrier."

Why – The Rest of the Story

Craig cocked his head and leaned in toward the two. "Are either of you familiar with the name Paul Harvey?"

Soni answered, "I am, Craig. He broadcast a radio program called 'The Rest of the Story,' which my family listened to when I was younger. It shared astonishing, true stories of both the famous and the unknown. And the listener never knew who the story was about until the end."

"Great recall, Soni. It premiered in the mid-1970s and featured over three thousand such stories during its lifetime. I mention him because there is a 'rest of the story' to *my* story."

"Are we going to need more tissues?" Cheri asked.

Craig winked. "You never know."

Soni reached for one. "I'll be prepared, just in case."

"Just after I turned thirty, I was showing property near the mission where I was adopted. I always wanted to learn who my birth mom was, so I walked in one day. They opened up their records, but most of the information was redacted. However, a few minor things weren't. I combined those few clues with the additional information I discovered at the county courthouse and began connecting the dots. I first discovered her family was from Memphis. More research led me to a dentist's office. It turned out to be her brother's. Thinking I was calling on a business matter, the receptionist gave me the number of another business where my birth mom worked. She wasn't in, so I left a message with my name, number, and company, but not the reason for my call."

Cheri spoke up, "You were afraid she might think it was a scam and not call you back?"

"I knew that was a possibility, Cheri, and I didn't want to take that chance. I needed to share something with her that only her real son would know. When my birth mom called, I explained this wasn't a real estate call. I asked if October 5, 1969, meant anything. It didn't."

"That was your date of birth, wasn't it?" Soni asked.

"Yes, ma'am, and it's understandable that after thirty years, it might have faded from her memory. Then I asked if she recalled signing a handwritten note giving up rights to Baby Boy Shipmon to the state of Texas. There was a long pause on the phone. 'Do you remember Baby Boy Shipmon?' I asked. I paused to catch my breath. 'I'm that baby boy.' She broke down in tears. I did, too. 'Oh, my God,' she shouted, 'you found me! You found me!' She was moved by the fact that I wanted to find her, and shocked that I was able to."

Both ladies wiped away tears. "It's so very beautiful," Cheri confided. "What happened next?"

"She feared flying, so she drove down from Memphis the very next day to reconnect. Bless her heart. She was so emotional. I introduced her to my family and her new grandkids. She met my adoptive parents. I showed her my business. It was a dream come true for both of us. We became, and still are, very close."

Soni anxiously inquired, "Do you know what happened to your real dad? Did he know about you? Did they marry?"

"He knew about me. I later got to meet him, but nothing ever came of it. And they never married. As for my birth mom, in time, she found the man of her dreams. They married and had two boys, whom I've met. I was quite jealous of them."

"Because she was able to be a mom to them?" Cheri gently asked.

"Not really. I was very happy for them. The fact that I'm only five foot eight and they're both six foot six with a full head of hair is what I was jealous of!" Both ladies chuckled.

"So, where is everyone now?" Soni asked.

"One is a professor and lives in Chicago. The other is a banker and resides in Memphis. And my birth mom? Well, she's now retired; she and her husband live in Florida."

Cheri interjected, "May I ask what she retired from?"

Craig grinned. "That's the *rest of the story.* My birth mom *and* my adoptive mom were *both* in real estate. Nature *and* nurture left me no choice. I was destined for this business. I have to believe they are the reason **Why** I'm here."

Soni spoke up, "That has to be one of the most touching stories ever. Thank you for opening up your heart to us."

"I agree with Soni. And now that we know *the rest of the story,* we understand *why* the **Why** Key and Serving Man are so important to you. A movie could be made about your life."

"If that were to happen," Craig added, "we know who will be cast for the lead role, right?" Together, everyone shouted "Mr. Clean!" as they high-fived to celebrate the moment.

WHY – YOUR VALUE PROPOSITION

Let's get back to our task at hand," Craig stated. "Soni, if you will turn the page, we'll discuss the last document titled YOUR VALUE PROPOSITION."

As she did so, she asked, "I take it this is also connected to our **Why** Key and Serving Man?"

"Yes, ma'am. Our *self*-management **Why** leads our people to *their* Big Why. It establishes why they are the best person to help a family with their real estate needs. And when they can help them, they are helping get **Where** *they* want to be. Soni, would you care to read the four points under the heading 'Your Value Proposition Defined'?"

"I'd be happy to. *1. It is a unique, memorable, and persuasive statement that expresses the true value of working with you. 2. Addresses the specific and special needs of the buyers and sellers in your market. 3. States what you will do for your client to earn your commission/fee. 4. Holds you accountable to high standards.* I like this. I like the clarity."

Cheri spoke up, "Me, too. It reminds me of something I used with my team from Spencer Johnson and Larry Wilson's book, *The One Minute Sales Person.* It introduced the idea of purpose, process, and payoff."

Craig responded, "Very similar, Cheri. And for this to be effective, it *must* be written down. They can't just think it and expect it to come out right. Here's why it must be reduced to writing first. A husband might want to say to his wife, 'When I look at you, dear, time stands still.' "

"What a beautiful message."

"It is. But when he actually says, *'You have a face that can stop a clock!'* we have a problem, right?" Both ladies roared.

"I would have felt tempted to slap him," Soni laughed.

"Most would agree. And you two likely agree we don't want our people slapped by not saying what they meant. Once they *see* it written down, they begin to *feel* it expressed. They can then massage, tweak, fine-tune, and perfect that initial draft. And after several drafts, they need to do several more. By then, they will have *internalized* it. Which means they're ready to *speak* it. They will need to recite it aloud, over . . . and over . . . and over, until it flows naturally off their tongue."

Cheri spoke, "My experience is that most aren't disciplined enough to write it on their own accord, which is where the mirrors at the **Who** Key come in. We can provide the accountability they need."

Their Secret Sauce

"The short yet powerful script they are perfecting here," Craig interjected, "is just one of many they will need to perfect. We have a total of forty-eight provided—from 'New to Real Estate' to 'Presenting a Counteroffer to the Buyer Agent' and everything in between."

"I take it they're not expected to memorize them," Soni clarified.

"Heavens, no. These are ideas. Samples. These provide a head start. They are expected to rewrite them in their *own* words, putting their personality, their *own* style into them."

"Just checking, Craig. Rolly set those expectations with us during our training. He gave us the tools to help us lay out everything we hoped our guests would experience—everything we hoped to do *and* say. '*Planned*—not canned,' he told us. There's a big difference."

"There is, Soni. The secret of a great chef is not in the spices they use but in the spice *they* put into what they create. It all comes together in the presentation they make when the final dish is presented. In the end, *they* are the secret sauce."

Cheri remarked, "I like the way you put that, Craig."

"Thank you. We are fortunate to have a lady on our team who loves helping our new agents find their secret sauce. Her name is Margo Villarreal. Like Sherri in **S.M.I.L.E.**, Margo was also a teacher. Because a large portion of our agents are Hispanic, as are many of our buyers and sellers, Margo's bilingualism is a huge plus. What one might say in English does not necessarily translate well into Spanish."

"Si, I see," Soni replied with a wink.

Craig grinned. "Perfect example, Soni. Margo is also involved with various volunteer groups. She has been on the Phone Duty Committee for ten years and counting. She is part of ALC—our Associate Leadership Council. In addition, she and several colleagues founded an Ambassadors Group to help fellow Realtors. They meet in this room every Tuesday morning. She loves being a mentor."

"Good for her, Craig. We need more Margos in the world. What prompted her to leave teaching? I know Sherri's reason."

"Her son. He had just graduated from the University of Texas in 2014 and chose a career in real estate. He asked his mom to join him, and much to his surprise, she did. They both got their license together and were a dynamic team at our brokerage for four incredible years."

"You say *were* a dynamic team. Something happened?"

Craig sighed, "Something happened, Soni. Her son passed away suddenly from an enlarged heart. It broke Margo's heart. It broke *our* hearts."

Soni glanced at Cheri. Both were in tears. "We're so saddened to hear that. What was her son's name?"

"Danny. Just like his father and his grandfather. Since Danny's passing, Margo tells us she sees cardinals in the windows of all the homes she shows. 'He is always with me,' she says. Danny is a big part of her **Why**. She derives great satisfaction from helping our young agents. She is in the mirrors of many. She is a big part of our *self*-management efforts here at Heritage."

"We never know what life is going to give us, do we?"

"We do not, Soni. One mother finds a son. Another loses a son. The circle of life. As Margo says, 'That's why we have to make every single moment of every single day count.' "

From Walls to Halls

Amen," Cheri responded, "*every* moment. Let's get back to *this* moment. The visual of Margo in the mirrors on the walls of so many young agents reminds me of something I learned from Rolly that inspired me to *hang* something in our halls. It stemmed from a book he recommended written by

Carl Sewell, *Customers for Life*. Carl owns car dealerships in Texas: Cadillac, Lexus, Chevrolet, and Hyundai. The customer satisfaction scores at his dealerships are the best in the auto industry. Oh, and so is profitability."

"That's a winning combination," Soni stated. "So, what does this have to do with halls?"

"Carl measures *everything* at his dealerships and posts the results for everyone to see. Carl says, 'People really like to know how they're doing. The more you post, the more effective it is.' When we began posting the results of everything we measured by category and by name for *all* to see in the hallways in our division office, we discovered he was right."

"Are we talking things like sales performance numbers, customer satisfaction, conversion and loss ratios, and such?"

"And more, Soni. Mortgage capture rate, profitability, contract accuracy, along with the percentages for every category of sales: referral, self-originated, walk-in, Internet, and Realtor. If we measured it, we posted it."

"I trust it wasn't done to embarrass anyone or put them on the spot."

"Just the opposite. It was to let everyone know how well they were performing in their profession. Think about it, Soni. Professional athletes are among the highest-paid professionals, and they are measured on *everything* they do. That's the only way they know if they are getting better or falling short of where they used to be or want to be. And the fact that their teammates, coaches, and even fans can also see where they are is a powerful motivator. It's a huge influence on their **Why**."

"When you think about it, the athletes who make the hall of fame in their respective sports typically have the most impressive numbers."

"They do, Soni. We referred to the postings on our walls as their 'Hall of Fame.' "

"I like that," Soni acknowledged. "And if that person has invited or accepted someone to be in their mirror, that person **Who** is helping or holding them accountable will know how well they are doing in *their* role."

"Precisely. It can serve to motivate them, too."

Craig spoke up, "I have a question about motivation. Who is motivated to call it a day and shift our discussion from walls to walks?"

Cheri smiled. "If you're talking about the River Walk, Craig, I'm all in."

"Count me in, too," Soni added. "I take it we're done for the afternoon?"

"Unless you have any questions about anything we covered," Craig responded.

"At the moment, no, sir. You two have done a remarkable job. If any do come to mind, we can discuss them over a frozen margarita. The best ones in Texas are served on the River Walk, Cheri!"

Cheri smiled. "I'll drink to that, Soni." She turned to address Craig. "Before we go, do we get that tour of your building you promised earlier?"

"Promise made, promise kept, Cheri. Let's take a break, and we'll meet back at the lobby. Restrooms are just around the corner behind the front desk.

Living His **Why**

The tour was everything the two expected, and then some. They walked 44,000 square feet of luxury office space, and saw all that draw the best and brightest agents: The high ceilings and an abundance of windows, giving it a bright, open, and modern feel. A kitchen and break area complementing each floor. Eighty-nine private offices reserved for the top producers. The facilities include event conference rooms, a production studio, collaborative spaces, private, closed, and ventilated pod workstations, as well as an in-house nutritionist. They even have a full-time porter who cleans the building and keeps the restrooms sparkling and sanitized.

The building serves as a hub for a team that sells over $3 billion in real estate annually. Ancillary businesses for mortgage and title services are housed here. Craig employs nineteen full-time staff members who provide support and training to the team. When he said he wanted his agents to have what he never had, he delivered on it. They are living his **Why**!

Following the tour, Craig accepted Cheri's offer to ride with her and Soni to the hotel. She could drop him back at his office on her way home. The three took advantage of the short drive to learn more about each other.

Cheri and Craig discovered that Soni entered and won a beauty contest during high school. Winning Miss Fort Stockton earned her a scholarship, which covered the cost of her first year of college.

Cheri and Soni learned that Craig enjoys snow skiing and fishing. But 'Craig style' of course—skiing in the Swiss Alps and salmon fishing in Alaska.

Blanketed by the shade of giant cypress trees towering ten stories above the river, the three enjoyed a delicious dinner of Mexican cuisine and frozen margaritas. Afterward, they took a three-minute walk to The Alamo. Cheri felt a chill run up her spine as she stood in awe of the old Spanish mission. Although a Florida girl, she had learned from a young age that 187 men valiantly held off over four thousand soldiers of the enemy for thirteen long days. She knew those precious days bought General Sam Houston the time needed to assemble an army that defeated Santa Anna six weeks later, allowing Texas to become *self*-governed—or, in Rolly's terms, *self*-managed. Why did she know all this? Because Cheri Crockett Bass is a direct descendant of Davy Crockett, the U.S. congressman from Tennessee, among the last to die in the battle.

On their way back to the hotel, Soni was thrilled to discover that Rolly had reserved a room for her with a private balcony overlooking the River Walk at the elegant Spanish-style Omni La Mansion del Rio. She had always dreamed of staying there. She appreciated Rolly's generosity. She also enjoyed the generosity of her chaperones. They booked a spa treatment for her the next morning before her noon flight to Phoenix. A line from a Joe Walsh hit song could best describe Soni's week: *"Life's been good to me so far."*

Section 6: NO ACCIDENT

A Reunion

As a black stretch limousine pulled up to the clubhouse of a prestigious active adult community in Northwest Phoenix, an energetic, fit, middle-aged man rushed to open the rear door. "Hello, Soni. Please allow me to help you," he smiled, extending his hand. "I'm Hal Looney. On behalf of Rick and Tiffany, it's truly our pleasure to have you as our guest."

Impressed with his authenticity, Soni smiled back as she extended her hand and stepped out. "My goodness, Hal. What a pleasure to meet you! Rolly told me that you and Rick are Oklahoma boys known for being Southern gentlemen. So, would a handshake or a hug suit you best? You do know I'm a West Texas girl, right?"

"I do. And that's an easy answer, Soni. We Okies *always* choose a hug—Texan or not," he winked, giving Soni a gentle embrace. "Before we go inside, I must apologize for not meeting you at the airport. Typically, Rick or I would do so since we both live close by. Yet, neither of us could reschedule our prior commitments. Tiffany wasn't an option as she drove in six hours from San Diego this morning. So, the three of us opted for a limo. I hope you found this alternative acceptable."

Soni rolled her eyes. "Acceptable? Was it ever! I took a selfie and sent it to my family and friends. I felt like royalty."

"To us, you are. Let's see if we can continue that royal treatment inside. Rick is completing a quick tour of the clubhouse with Tiffany, and they should be joining us shortly. Allow me to grab your carry-on."

Hal escorted Soni to a library room he had reserved for their visit. A round table with four chairs was set in the center of the room. Soni noticed a large, laminated printout of the ***Self*-Management Model of Empowerment** in the center of the table, along with a two-inch-tall toy replica of a Radio Flyer Tricycle. *I can't wait to discover what that's about!* she thought as she hung her handbag on the chair facing the door. Hal placed her carry-on under a side table stocked with refreshments.

"Soni, please help yourself to the snacks and treats. As for the beverages, I learned you prefer unsweetened tea. Since I don't know your brand preference, I've selected six options for you. I hope you don't struggle with making decisions. Which one may I have the honor of serving you?"

"I don't struggle at all, Hal. I'll have the Gold Peak—my favorite. And you may have become my favorite server."

"I'm honored. Since this also happens to be my favorite, I'll join you." He placed hers, along with a glass of ice, at the seat she had selected while placing his at the seat to her left.

"Hal, the royalty thing is still working. I like the way you make people feel important."

"Excellent, Soni. You let me know if I start slipping."

"I've got a feeling that's not going to happen. It's obvious you pay attention to the *little* details."

"What makes you say that?"

"I notice you only offered six teas as opposed to . . . let's say . . . twenty-four," she stated with a grin. "I'm not the only one who notices the *little* details. The 'jars of jam' discussion from the ***S*** in **S.M.I.L.E.**, right?"[14]

"Ma'am, you're spot on."

"You know, Hal, I hope I enjoy my time with Rick and Tiffany as much as I'm enjoying my time with you."

At that moment, those two entered the room. "Soni, you're about to have the opportunity to see how that unfolds. It's my pleasure to introduce you to my *very* dear friends. I'll begin with the one I've known since we were kids. Soni Graves, this distinguished guy is Rick Andreen. He's the brainchild behind this property, which is sold out. He's created many other properties like this that we've developed over the years. He began his career in the industry as a builder at the age of twenty-three. From there, he moved into sales, sales management, and operations, eventually becoming the CEO and COO of two national companies outside our industry. You name it, he's done it. He's recently retired."

"Quadruple wow!" Soni exclaimed. "Wow, to this property. It's gorgeous. Wow, for your many accomplishments. They're impressive. Wow, to meeting you. I'm honored. And wow on your retirement. Congratulations. You look so youthful, as does Hal. There must be something in the Oklahoma water. Hal tells me you boys north of the Red River

---

[14] As part of her research in 2000, Dr. Sheena Iyengar, a professor at Columbia Business School, set up a tasting booth with a variety of gourmet jams at an upscale grocery store. Sometimes the booth had six flavors, and sometimes twenty-four, with the goal of seeing if the number of choices affected the number of jars of jam sold. Though a higher percentage of shoppers stopped to sample jam when offered twenty-four varieties, only three percent made a purchase. But of shoppers who stopped when offered only six jam varieties, thirty percent made a purchase. The conclusion? Too many options make choosing more difficult.

prefer hugs to handshakes," she stated, extending her arms. "Did he mislead me?"

"No, ma'am," Rick smiled as they exchanged hugs. "It's an honor to meet you, Soni. And thank you for all the 'wows'—especially the *youthful* one—although my receding hairline might say otherwise. Talking about wows, since I've known Tiffany the longest, with Hal's permission, I'd like to have the privilege of introducing her."

Receiving a nod from Hal, Rick continued, "Soni, it's my privilege to have you meet Tiffany Torgan. This dynamo of a lady was a rock star for the years we were all part of Rolly's team in Dallas in the early '90s. She is now the broker/owner of Prestige Properties of La Jolla, which is just north of San Diego, California. Though Tiffany, as you can witness, looks like a movie star who *never* ages, she's actually a TV star. She has appeared as a real estate expert on numerous HGTV Home & Garden programs and *all* the San Diego news channels."

Soni turned to address Tiffany. "I don't mean to sound like a broken record, but wow again! Tiffany, you're a heavy hitter for a person of such small stature, and you also look so young." Soni extended her arms for a hug as they embraced. "And I appreciate you driving six hours to meet with me. I'm sure you could be doing a lot back home. This alone speaks volumes about you."

"Thank you, Soni, on all accounts. It turns out this get-together serves as a reunion for the three of us. We understand from Rolly that you're a heavy hitter, too. We've all been excited to meet *you*! Before we move on, has anyone mentioned

Hal's background and accomplishments to you? He's so humble, I doubt he shared anything about himself."

"You're right, Tiffany. He is, and no, ma'am, he didn't."

"Then I'd be happy to. Fresh out of college, Hal was in commercial real estate in Atlanta. In 1991, he was asked to join our team in Dallas, a year after I did. Much like Rick, Hal has worn many hats in his career, all successfully. He is now the area president for the company that built this magnificent property. Hal oversees their operations in six communities for all of Arizona and Nevada. I understand three more are currently in the works."

"Impressive, Hal. *All* of you, impressive!" Soni added. "Now that I know the three of you worked for Rolly, I'm curious to know if you were all trained by him?"

Hal responded, "He was our boss in title only. We all felt we worked *with* him—not *for* him." Rick and Tiffany nodded in agreement. "As for training? Yes, ma'am. Rolly trained Rick and Tiffany. They, in turn, trained me."

"That's interesting. May I ask how that came about?" Soni questioned. "Is that appropriate for us to discuss?"

"It's most appropriate, Soni, after we set the stage for this afternoon's discussion. Before we all take our seats, may I suggest we check that our phones are on 'Respectful Mode'? And Tiffany, you and Rick might help yourself to the refreshments. As you can see, Soni and I already have."

"Hal, you are the consummate host," Tiffany stated as she took a seat across the table from Soni.

"And thanks for the reminder with the phones," Rick added as he took a seat to Soni's right.

Hal smiled and took the remaining seat. "You both are welcome. So, let's get started." He pointed to the ***Self-*** **Management Model** on the table. "Though our focus this afternoon is on the **How** and **Who** Keys and their Serving Men, you realize we'll be touching on *all* of them. And since we all have been 'empowered' by Rolly to decide how we address them, we felt it appropriate also to explore how events of the past led to this idea of *self*-management and the empowerment model that lies before us."

Tiffany interjected, "We all know Rolly well enough to realize he didn't wake up one day and all this just magically happened. During a call we had after Rolly asked us to come together for this visit, the three of us identified events that we believe helped lead him, and *all* of us, to where we are today."

Rick spoke up, "In addition, I'm certain we all appreciate that more goes into creating a *self*-managed team than just applying the Six Keys and their Serving Men. We're confident the stories we're about to share contain valuable lessons that have helped us, and we believe they can benefit you as well. Are you okay with our approach?"

"More than okay," Soni agreed. She then pointed to the miniature tricycle and grinned. "As long as this tricycle is a part of that discussion."

Tiffany smiled. "It's a *big* part that ties into the hiring of Hal and me. Plus, it has become a part of the ***Self-*** **Management Program**."

Soni removed her portfolio from her handbag and placed it on the table. "I can't wait to hear about all this. Where do we start?"

A Mindset of Excellence and Help

How about from the beginning?" Rick answered. "In 1990, Rolly accepted the position of VP of sales for the Dallas Northeast Division of a national homebuilder. He inherited eleven salespeople: ten seasoned veterans and one rookie. I was the new kid on the block. Although Rolly lacked formal management training, with no sales manager to learn from when he sold, the year before his arrival he was presented with the opportunity to fill two roles in his division in Central Texas. He sold on the weekends and managed the other salespeople during the week. He excelled at both."

"I've known Rolly for twenty-four years and never knew that," Soni responded. "I'm enjoying this. Please continue."

"Our division was one of three in the DFW area, and forty-two in the country. We were doing okay, enjoying a good market. That said, we had plenty of room for improvement. Our goal for that decade was to grow, and we were primed for that to happen. We had an overabundance of homesites on the ground and the opportunity to acquire more developed communities. We had a construction crew that could easily build more homes. And in eight of our ten neighborhoods, we had more traffic than our sales team could serve."

"Most interesting," Soni interjected. "Please continue."

"In addition, our models had two sales offices, but only one was double-staffed. We needed salespeople, and Rolly was tasked with hiring and training them, as well as managing the existing team. Our previous manager had a wealth of experience, but managed from behind his desk. We seldom saw him in the field."

"Unfortunately, that's often the norm," Soni remarked.

"Fortunately, that was not Rolly. He was hands-on."

"Excuse me," Hal interrupted with a grin. "You mean *wings*-on." Everyone laughed.

"Thank you, Hal, I stand corrected. *Wings*-on! At our Monday morning sales meeting, our division president introduced Rolly and explained that he was here to help us grow. Rolly shared two things with the team that morning. First, he was committed to excellence. He had high expectations of us and set the bar for our division to become the best sales team in the entire company, not just in the city. He emphasized that nothing short of excellence would be acceptable for the current team and those he would be hiring. Second, he told us he was there to help us. He emphasized that we would be working together *with* him. He committed to spending his time *with* us, *in* our neighborhoods, helping us *all* get better."

"That's powerful," Soni stated. "How was that message received?"

"With only three months of experience and no training, I was inspired! My senior counterparts? Not at all. They had been in sales far longer than Rolly. And because most were selling newer products in premium locations with a lot of traffic, they were making a lot of money. In some locations, they were taking orders. That was not the case for me. I had an older product in a less desirable area. Following the meeting, I took Rolly up on his offer for help. I had an issue with an available home I inherited that was having a birthday."

"Birthdays for available homes are not a good thing! What was his response?"

"He walked that home with me that afternoon."

"Good for him. And good for you," Tiffany remarked. "I'm not at all surprised. He was always there for me when I needed him. So, what was the problem with the home?"

"Do any of you recall the scene in the movie *Close Encounters of the Third Kind* where the lead actor builds a mud replica of Devil's Tower in his living room?"

"I do," Tiffany replied. "That was wild! Why do you ask?"

"In the kitchen, ants had built an almost identical replica of that tower. It started from a roof leak long before I got there and grew to a height of almost five feet."

"Did you say . . . five *feet*?" Soni grew wide-eyed. "Ants alive! So, what was Rolly's reaction? Was he upset? I know I would have flapped *my* wings if I'd had any!"

"If he was, he remained unruffled. He calmly asked how long the issue had been there and if I'd requested that construction fix the leak and remove the mound. I replied that I went all the way to the head of construction, who told me he would fix it after I sold it."

Hal shook his head. "Sadly, a somewhat typical response from construction in those days. What did Rolly do?"

"He put his wing tip to his chin, turned around, and strutted away for a moment. I could tell he was weighing his options. When he returned, he asked me to call that gentleman to come there immediately. When he arrived, Rolly began with a simple question: 'Does our division president know about this?' The answer was no. 'Would you like him *never* to know?' Embarrassed, the man replied he would be grateful if that did not happen. 'Then how soon can this be taken care of?' 'By the end of the week,' he responded. 'Do that, and this stays between us,' Rolly assured him."

"I'm anxious to know what happened," Soni quizzed.

"Rolly met all of us back at the home on Friday afternoon. It was pristine. He thanked his counterpart for honoring his word. The man thanked Rolly for honoring his. They became, and remained, good friends. Oh, and I sold the home that weekend!"

"Beautiful story, Rick,' Soni exclaimed. "So, what did *you* learn, and what can *we* learn from this?"

"We could make a case study of this if we had the time, Soni. First, set a standard of excellence with your team, understanding that excellence extends beyond our work. It applies to *everyone* involved with the product or service offered. Be the best you can be, and hold everyone to that standard."

Hal began scrolling through the messages on his phone. "Rick knows my love for racing. Recently, a friend saw a sign at a racetrack that caught his attention. It was so impactful that he took a picture to share with me, which I then shared with my team. Y'all might appreciate it, too." Finding it, he turned his phone so the others could read:

> SOMEWHERE AT THIS TRACK, THERE IS A LITTLE KID THAT WANTS TO BE JUST LIKE YOU SOMEDAY. YOU OWE IT TO THEM TO BE THE BEST YOU CAN BE!

"What a compelling interpretation of excellence!" Soni responded. "Would you please forward that to me? I want to share it with my team." Hal nodded.

"How about me, too?" Tiffany requested. "Rick and Hal know I *love* quotes. I memorized my favorite one about excellence from Vince Lombardi. 'The quality of a person's life is in direct proportion to their commitment to *excellence*, regardless of their chosen field of endeavor.' "

"One worth remembering, Tiffany. Believe it or not, his name came up earlier this week," Soni shared.

"Not surprising," Hal remarked. "His life and career were about excellence. You know, the longer I live, the more I'm convinced that excellence is found in the DNA of *everyone* who either is or desires to become *self*-managed. *Self*-managed individuals want to be the best they can be, and they hold themselves to that standard."

"I agree," Soni stated. "I'm confident we would also agree that if Rolly could have a 'do-over'—knowing what he knows now—that at that very first meeting, he would have set the expectation that his *ultimate* goal was to empower everyone on the team to become *self*-managed."

"You're right, Soni. He only knew what he knew at the time. We must continually strive to find more effective ways to do everything. That's how we all got to this," Hal concluded as he pointed at the ***Self*-Management Model**.

"I wholeheartedly agree," Rick confirmed. "The second lesson is to build a foundation of trust. If you say you're there to help others, help them! Trust is what earns us the right to be in their mirrors at the **Who** Key."

Soni added, "It was certainly at the heart of everything Ester and Rob, Karen and Vicky, and Cheri and Craig did."

"Third, don't burn bridges—*build* them. Rolly built a bridge with those who were responsible for building our homes. When our sales numbers began to skyrocket, we needed a construction team that was there for us, and they were. And the relationships we had with purchasing, mortgage, title, and our vendors were all just as crucial."

"Powerful takeaways," Soni affirmed. "I love that story."

"Good, because I told you that one, to tell you this one."

One Good Turn Deserves Another

Following this experience, I sensed Rolly and I had a special connection. I could trust him," Rick acknowledged, "and he could trust me. As a result, I felt comfortable giving him a copy of a new business book I'd just begun reading."

"That required an immense amount of faith on your part, Soni sensed. "He easily could have taken that as an insult or you meddling with his management style."

"It was a risk, for sure. But one I'm thankful I took."

"Aren't we all," Hal stated. Tiffany nodded in agreement.

"The book is *The Seven Habits of Highly Effective People,* isn't it?" Soni surmised. "Rolly reveals the worn-out, tattered pages in all his training. Dr. Covey's book certainly stands unique."

"That it does, and we'll get back to that book in a bit. Our situation was also unique, as Rolly and I shared another commonality in the area of our business development. We had needs: I needed him, and he needed me. Let me explain. With his success in teaching and applying the selling process that helped make him and others successful, I needed him."

"Turns out we all did," Tiffany remarked. Soni and Hal nodded.

"Respectfully, I also knew he needed me. He needed someone on his team who was eager to learn and would apply what he brought to the table. *I* was that person."

Hal spoke up, "At one time, I recall you shared with me that the seasoned salespeople had been through the same training he received and snubbed their noses at it."

"That's true, Hal. And Rolly was well aware of this."

"So, how did someone who was committed to excellence, to helping his team get better, deal with that?" Soni inquired.

"He chose not to annoy the pig," Rick answered.

"Excuse me? He chose what?" Soni felt a bit flabbergasted.

"Remember, I told you it was a good market. Since we were making our numbers, he decided for the time being to leave well enough alone. He chose to focus on training me and the new folks he would be hiring. He anticipated that our success would cause the others to change their position on the value of the training eventually."

"Did it?" Soni inquired.

"We're about to find out."

"So, what do 'pigs' have to do with this?"

"It comes from a Mark Twain quote. 'Never try to teach a pig to sing. It wastes your time and annoys the pig!' "

"Now that's funny!" Soni laughed. "I can *so* relate to where he's coming from."

"To address the staffing needs, Rolly began interviewing candidates immediately. Over the next two months, he hired four salespeople—three of whom had extensive sales experience. Of those three, one proved to be a home run. He adopted the company's selling system and outperformed the existing senior staff. The other two didn't make it."

"Hiring experienced people can be a time-saver when it works out," Soni responded. "They can hit the ground running. But great ones are hard to find and are rarely on the market. Rolly can count his blessings that one panned out. So, what about the fourth? I take it he or she had no sales experience. And if so, how did he or she do?"

"It was a she," Rick replied with a smile, pointing to his right. "It was *this* she," he admitted. "May I suggest you ask Tiffany how she did?"

"Oh, I'm *absolutely* loving this!" Soni exclaimed as she addressed Tiffany. "When does your story begin?"

A Young Sherri

I met Rolly two months after Rick's 'close encounter' with the ant mound. After earning my degree in economics from Texas A&M, I took a job with a major employer in Northeast Dallas."

"Good for you. My daughter, Ashton, is pursuing the same degree from A&M. What a coincidence."

"It is, Soni. That degree got me my first job. But instincts soon told me something wasn't right with my manager. He turned out to be creepy, so I resigned and immediately began searching for another job, any job near where I lived. I was determined not to ask my parents for help. The Medieval Inn, a nearby restaurant, was the only place hiring. So, I became a waitress."

Soni smiled at her new friend in encouragement.

"The official job title was a 'wench,' where we all wore Medieval costumes," Tiffany explained.

"I admire that, Tiffany. Sometimes, life requires us to take a step backward to move forward. I've been there."

"Looking back, I'm thankful I took that job. It confirmed many things for me: if I treated people with respect, made them feel important, and got them smiling and laughing, I would not only get more enjoyment out of what I was doing, but would also be rewarded with big tips, repeat customers, and lots of referrals."

"Sounds like the philosophy of **S.M.I.L.E.** So, how did you end up interviewing with Rolly?"

"I had a friend whom he had trained who knew he was hiring. To my good fortune, Rolly's office was near where I lived. Despite having no sales experience, I reached out to Rolly."

"Obviously, the interview went well, but I'm curious what took place. Our industry tends only to hire experienced people. What made Rolly take a chance on you?"

"Good question, Soni. I attribute it to several things. For starters, I feel that being referred was important. Someone Rolly had trained and was successful felt I would be a good fit. Rolly trusted his recommendation. That got me in the door."

"It's gotten a lot of people in my door."

"During the interview, Rolly pointed to a stack of résumés on his desk—several dozen. 'These are résumés of experienced salespeople who want to work here,' he stated. Then he referenced mine. 'Tiffany, you don't have any new home experience. Tell me why I should hire you.' "

"Rolly can be straightforward at times. Were you rattled?"

"Not at all," Tiffany confided. "I looked him in the eyes and confidently replied, 'There are two reasons, sir: I bring no bad habits with me. *And* I'm willing to do whatever you teach me. I'll never question whether it will work. I'll do it. I'm grateful you're even considering me and would be honored to be trained by you and become a part of your team.' "

"I would have hired you on the spot."

Tiffany smiled. "He did. He later confided that the biggest factor influencing his decision was my character . . . my values . . . who I was. He appreciated that I trusted my instincts in my previous job, explaining that instinct is something he cannot teach. He was also impressed with my work ethic as I refused to ask my parents to bail me out. Plus, he admired my humility, that I was willing to take a job many might think was 'beneath' them, to eventually get where I wanted to be."

Rick interrupted, "If I might jump in. He also told me he was impressed with her attitude. He was convinced she wanted to learn and was willing to take direction."

Soni remarked, "That was the first thing he required of Sherri if he was going to help her learn to **S.M.I.L.E.**"

Rick added, "And just like Sherri, she kept her promise, being 'who' she is. After Rolly trained her, she joined the other new salesperson and me as top performers in the division. We won all the contests and trips. We received all the awards. We were honored at all the dinners."

"Good for y'all. I'm curious to know how the senior people reacted to this. The ones who felt they didn't need the training. Did they ever come around?"

A Taste of Empowerment

I'm glad you asked," Rick answered. "After the senior group was dominated quarter after quarter by us 'newbies,' Rolly received a call from them, requesting a private meeting with him."

"The backseat can prove humbling," Soni stated.

"It can. They expressed frustration with the newcomers, whether experienced or new to the industry, who were winning everything. They shared that, at first, they attributed it to luck, but soon realized the newbies' performance was a result of embracing and applying his training. So, they asked Rolly to take them through the training again."

"And naturally, he honored their request."

Tiffany grinned. "He did, but not quite the way they expected. Because the training was divided into modules of specific components of the selling process, Rolly asked if we, the newcomers, would be interested in conducting the training. We were excited and honored. We divvied up the modules and he trained *us* on how to train *them*. We loved it."

"Good for y'all. And good for him. He trusted you and empowered *all* of you."

"That he did. And it was a win-win all the way around. Did the seasoned people become better? Absolutely! The playing field had been leveled. But something unexpected occurred. When the student became the teacher, they improved. As a result, *everyone's* numbers increased. Over the three years Rolly was there, our sales grew from under three hundred before he arrived, to over eight hundred by the time he moved on to take over the company's national training."

"If I might add," Hal interjected, "by the time I came on board, less than a year after Tiffany's story, quite a number of the seasoned folks became involved in helping train me. The culture of the entire team had undergone a significant change. It became a culture of 'we' and of 'excellence.' "

"You're right, Hal. Many immediately volunteered to help, and *they* loved it. You just mentioned you coming on board. Earlier, I proposed that our tricycle had a lot to do with the hiring of you *and* me. Since Rick was instrumental in you joining the team, it's only fitting he shares your story."

The Tricycle

Thank you, Tiffany. Despite Hal's temporary lapse of judgment, choosing to go to Oklahoma State as opposed to *my* University of Oklahoma, we stayed in touch."

Hal snickered. "Hey, I just thought I could relate more to being a 'Cowboy' instead of a 'Sooner'—whatever the heck a 'Sooner' is!"

Rick smiled. "Hal was aware that the Dallas market was recovering from the '80s savings and loan fiasco better than Atlanta, so he reached out to me to see if we were hiring. I was excited. I immediately approached Rolly to set up a phone call for an interview. I assured him that Hal would be a valuable addition to our team."

"I'm certain that went well," Soni surmised.

"Not hardly. Rolly responded that he had no interest in speaking to Hal, nor interviewing him."

"Seriously!" Soni remarked as she glanced at Hal. He shrugged his shoulders. "What was your reaction, Rick?"

"I dug in my heels. I pointed out that Hal came from a good family with solid values and a strong work ethic. I described him as smart, honest, caring, and a team player. I trusted his character. I emphasized his positive attitude, thirst for learning, and willingness to take direction. I reiterated my belief that he would be extremely successful."

"Good for you. With that strong of a recommendation, Rolly had to agree with your request, right?"

"Wrong! Once again, he stated he had no interest in speaking with Hal or interviewing him. I was distraught. Candidly, I struggled to maintain my composure. Frustrated, I asked what I should tell Hal as I owed him a call."

"I'm on pins and needles," Soni said. "What did he say?"

"Rolly told me to ask Hal how soon he could get to Dallas. He said to tell him he didn't *need* to interview or speak to him. Tell him he has a job!"

"That's amazing, Rick. Did you ask why he didn't need to interview or talk to Hal?"

"I did, Soni. Rolly slid his copy of *The Seven Habits* in front of me, which I had given him a year earlier. 'You're a big believer in this book,' he stated, 'so am I. Without anyone's permission, we've incorporated it into what we teach our sales team, and it's making a profound difference for them, both professionally and personally. The answer is in this book."

Hal scratched his head. "Whoa. I thought *The Seven Habits* had always been a part of the training."

"Far from it. Rolly, Tiffany, and I felt that if we asked permission to integrate its teachings into the curriculum, our request would be rejected. We trusted our success would speak for itself if it ever became an issue. And we were successful.

We became the top sales team in the country for our company!"

Soni spoke up, "I'm not at all surprised. Sometimes being willing to ask for forgiveness is a better strategy than asking for permission."

"Exactly!" Rick confirmed. "By the time the three of us, including Rolly, had moved on to pursue other opportunities, every executive VP and division president in the company flew to Provo, Utah, to personally attend Dr. Covey's program. Me included! And it's worth mentioning, they also all flew to Dallas to learn what we were doing that worked so well. From those visits, salesperson after salesperson was recruited from our team to lead other sales teams. We were proud of that!" Tiffany and Hal proudly nodded.

"I'd say your gamble *and* Rolly's commitment to excellence paid off."

"Big time, Soni. So, back to the book. Rolly flipped to the dog-eared page where Dr. Covey emphasized the importance of *character ethic*, concluding with his statement that 'Only basic goodness gives life to technique.' "

"Rolly still quotes that page in his training," Soni stated.

"And likely always will. He shared that he witnessed that character ethic in me, as well as in Tiffany, and all the other successful people we hired and trained. 'If you see that in Hal,' he told me, 'then we need him here immediately!' "

Soni smiled and pointed to the tricycle. "That's quite an interesting story, Rick. Are we about to get to this?"

"We are." Rolly turned to the page that revealed three circles: one of 'Knowledge' or '*What* to do'; one of 'Skills' or '*How* to do'; and a third of 'Desire' or '*Want* to do.' "

"Having read the book, I seem to recall where the three overlap; a habit is formed. Is that correct?"

"It is, Soni. Good memory! The fact that they're all the same size leaves one to believe they're all equal in importance. But Rolly, being Rolly, questioned if they were equal. Soni, do you have an opinion on their equality?"

"I do, and I don't, Rick. I *do* have an opinion. I *don't* believe they're all equal. I think 'Desire' or '*Want* to do' is the most important and should be larger."

"We agree," Hal responded. "Since Rolly has always encouraged us to look at things from a different perspective, practicing what he preached, he looked at the three circles differently." Hal handed the tricycle replica to Soni. "Rolly saw these three circles as the wheels of a tricycle. Of the three, which do you feel is the most important and why?"

"That's easy, Hal, the front wheel," Soni confidently answered, spinning it while also steering the handlebars from side to side. "It provides both momentum *and* direction."

"You're right. We'll come back to the 'direction' part shortly. For now, let's focus on momentum—on moving this tricycle forward. Rolly equated Covey's 'Desire' to 'Attitude.' That understood, what do the back wheels serve as?"

"Comfort. Stability. Support. They help it more easily get where we want it to go," Soni replied, pushing it across the table toward Tiffany. "I'm betting he saw the back wheels as 'Knowledge' and 'Skills'—Covey's other two circles."

"And you would win that bet," Tiffany affirmed, catching it and turning it around. "Now, a most important question. Which of the three wheels *cannot* be taught?"

"The front wheel of attitude."

"You got it! Now, with all the importance of that front wheel, let's go back to something Rolly also saw in Rick and me. A quality he mentioned that Rick saw in Hal. You recall what it was?"

"Character ethic?" Soni guessed.

"Yes, ma'am. And the *seat* on our tricycle represents character ethic," Tiffany stressed as she touched the seat with her finger. "It represents the person who will determine what the tricycle will be used *for.* Good or evil? Constructive or destructive? Justice or injustice? Right or wrong?" She gently pushed the tricycle back to Soni.

"That's profound!" Soni caught it again. "Now I understand the significance of this small toy." She touched each part as she continued, "Attitude, direction, values, knowledge, and skills *all* come together right here."

"And interestingly enough," Tiffany added, "three of the five parts *cannot* be trained—the front wheel, the handlebars, and the seat. They can only be hired."

"Am I to gather that the three of you are suggesting this toy can be used as a hiring tool?"

Rick answered, "Not *can* be, Soni. It *must* be." Hal and Tiffany nodded in agreement. "If we're hiring people because of their knowledge and skills while disregarding their values, attitude, and willingness to take direction, that decision is guaranteed to come back to bite us."

"I see that now. Unfortunately, that's happened to me more than once, I'm sad to say."

"It has likely happened to everyone in a hiring role, Soni, and to us included. But, if we begin with finding a person with the *right* values, a *good* attitude, and a *willingness* to take direction, we can teach the knowledge and skills they need to do their job, provided we have the right training."

"And that 'right' training," Hal responded, "includes teaching them how to become *self*-managed."

"I recognize that now more than ever," Soni confided. At that moment, she noticed a young man she recognized from the front desk enter the room and hand Hal a note. Reading it, Hal discreetly slipped out of the room.

Rick added, "It's been our experience—our being the three of us, plus the others you have spoken with this week—that people with the right values, a good attitude, and a willingness to take direction relish the notion of *self*-management and empowerment."

Tiffany pointed to the ***Self*-Management Model of Empowerment** display. "Which is why we felt the stories we shared of how Rolly's experiences led him and us here might be of value in helping you create a *self*-managed team."

"Will they ever! I see a use for everything shared," Soni confessed. Pointing to the tricycle, she continued, "And this little toy has opened my eyes to some things I can do better."

Tiffany smiled, "Just so you know, we are nowhere near done with it." She reached out to pat Rick's hand. "Let's see where Rick takes us."

Then and Now

As Rick was about to respond, Hal reentered the room accompanied by a tall blonde whose mere presence radiated excellence. The lady saw Rick and dashed to hug him.

"Please excuse the interruption!" Hal exclaimed. "I was just handed a note that a dear friend discovered Rick and I were here and asked if she could say hello."

"And I'm glad she did!" Rick shared in disbelief. "Kelly Young. My, what a pleasant surprise! Do you have time to join us? You'd fit right in with our discussion of *self*-management. You took care of your business like it was nobody's business."

"That's what I was taught and expected to do, Rick. And yes, sir, I do have a few minutes," Kelly excitedly responded. "My business partner and I are about to meet with one of my past homeowners who asked us to list her home. I got here early, and when I learned that you and Hal were here, I had to find you." She turned to Tiffany and Soni. "Please forgive me for interrupting. These two gentlemen taught me everything I needed to know about *self*-management. They've made a *huge* impact on my life."

Tiffany responded, "I could say the same thing, Kelly. I'm Tiffany Torgan, and this is Soni Graves. Based on how you greeted Rick, I take it you're a hugger?"

"Big time!" Kelly replied as she embraced both ladies. "It's a pleasure to meet the two of you."

"It's our pleasure, Kelly," Soni responded. "And congrats on the listing appointment. I take it you're no longer selling new homes?"

"I'm not, Soni. Thirteen years ago, my husband and I decided to prioritize motherhood over livelihood, so I became a stay-at-home mom for our three boys, who were one, three, and five years old at the time. Now that they're teenagers, I got into general real estate four years ago. It gives me the flexibility to still interact with them and resume my career."

Hal put his arm around Kelly's shoulder. "For the ten years before that, Kelly was a top producer with us. We hated to lose her, but understood their decision. It's the struggles and non-negotiables Karen and Vicky shared with all of us. It's life, and we have to live our lives as we see fit."

"You're right, Hal. I wanted to be involved in their early school years, volunteering where I could and just being there. I've never regretted that decision and was so grateful for the support and encouragement you and Rick gave us as I made that transition. And who knows? After the youngest graduates, I might be interested in rejoining your team."

"I would look forward to that conversation, Kelly!" Hal grinned.

Rick spoke up, "Your story of how you were determined to become a part of our team the *first* time inspired so many. Would you mind sharing it with these ladies while we all take a seat?" He retrieved a chair and positioned it between him and Soni.

"I'd love to," Kelly responded.

Before Hal took his seat, he served Kelly a glass of sparkling water over ice. "I'm hoping this is still your favorite."

"You never cease to amaze me," Kelly smiled.

"Please, amaze us now by your story," Hal replied.

"After growing up in Springfield, Missouri, I went to Seattle Pacific University in Queen Anne, Washington, just outside Seattle. I wanted a change of scenery, and I got it! After graduating, my passion for people and building relationships led me to a sales role with Xerox. My future was bright, but the weather wasn't. I missed sunshine. So, I transferred to Phoenix."

Soni responded, "Our family vacations here each spring to go golfing. I'd say you got your sunshine."

"Did I ever!" Kelly smiled as she rolled her eyes. "As much as I loved sales, I came to realize my heart would never be passionate about copiers or fax machines. What I loved was homes and interior design, so I got my real estate license and applied with the brand Rick started. In my opinion, it was then, and still is, the best homebuilding operation in the valley."

Tiffany said, "I felt the same way when applying for a sales position where Rolly and Rick were. I had no new home sales experience either, but was determined to make it happen."

"Good for you, Tiffany. I couldn't get in front of the manager there at the time, so I dropped off my résumé and followed up with a phone call. After leaving several messages, she finally called me back. But, with my lack of new home experience, she had no interest in interviewing me."

"Hal knows what that feels like," Soni remarked as he looked at him and winked. "So, what did you do, Kelly?"

"I knew if I was going to *make* a difference in this industry, I was going to have to *be* different. I bought a beautiful candle from a Hallmark store, wrapped it in a colorful bow, and changed my cover letter. In all caps, I wrote . . . I'M READY TO SET THE WORLD ON FIRE IN NEW HOME SALES!" Soni and Tiffany cheered. "That got me the interview."

Hal smiled. "An interview with five people on our team—me being the last. Yes, she had an impressive track record with Xerox. But that's not what got her the job."

"So, what did?" Tiffany anxiously inquired.

"Caring," Hal answered. "I always like to ask people what they are most proud of in their lives during an interview." He turned to address Kelly. "Would you share your answer with Tiffany and Soni?"

"Sure. Some of my favorite memories as a young girl were playing kickball barefoot with kids in the neighborhood, catching lightning bugs, and riding my bike. One of my best friends lived a couple of streets away. He was a special needs kid. The other kids made fun of him and would leave him out of our games. *They* called him retarded. *I* called him my friend. I had a cool connection with him because he loved riding his bike. I cherished my time with him and riding our ten-speeds. When I moved to another part of town, I was so sad, hoping he would be okay without me. I cared. When I entered high school, I would often find someone eating alone in the cafeteria and sit down to talk with them over lunch. I've always cared about people and wanted them to feel important and appreciated. I guess that's just who I was. As a young girl, one of my favorite quotes was from Mark Twain. 'Kindness is the language the deaf can hear and the blind can see.' "

Soni placed one hand on Kelly's arm as she reached for a tissue with the other. "I love you! And I just met you. You are a special lady. I would have hired you in a heartbeat!" Tiffany nodded. Soni then pointed to the tricycle. "We're back to the seat, the front wheel, and the handlebars, aren't we? Character ethic, attitude, and direction!"

"That we are," Rick answered. "The training we provided of putting people first, of caring, of making others feel important—the philosophy of **S.M.I.L.E.**—just brought out the best of who Kelly was."

"Empowering me to become *self*-managed was perhaps the *best* thing you and Hal did for me," Kelly confided.

Hal responded, "Thank you, Kelly. Do you have time to share my favorite story about empowerment when you brought everybody together to solve a problem? The one that reminded me of the scene from the movie *Apollo Thirteen* when they gathered the engineers in one room and spread out *everything* they had to work with on a table to get the air filtration system working. The line was 'We have to figure out a way to fit *this* . . . in the hole for *this* . . . using nothing but *that.*' And the only acceptable outcome was finding a solution that would get the three astronauts safely home."

"From tricycles to space travel," Soni stated with a grin. "Ya'll are certainly keeping this interesting."

Tiffany spoke up, "I'm interested in hearing this, too."

Kelly glanced at her watch. "I have time for this *one* story. I had been dancing with a couple who fell in love with everything about this place. It turns out they owned several homes throughout the country and weren't sure how to make this one work. It was late in the evening, and they and their Realtor agreed to return the next morning. When they arrived, I had invited our mortgage loan officer, Pam Hackett, to attend so she could help find the ideal loan. I also invited Evelyn Saracco, our VP of sales, to tap into her expertise. When I learned that the couple always ran everything by their financial advisor, we also got him on the phone. With everyone present and accounted for, I asked the couple a question I already knew the answer to . . . 'You want to own a home here, don't you?' Their reply was 'Absolutely. More than anything.' To that, I responded, 'Then we're not leaving here until we *all* figure out a way to make it happen. *We* will get you into this home!' "

Soni responded, "And you did, didn't you?"

Kelly grinned from ear to ear. "We did, Soni."

Hal spoke up, "I've got two questions that Soni might like to know the answer to. Had you ever done this before? And, did you need to get permission from your VP or anyone else to try this approach?"

"No, sir, and no, sir. I had never tried this before. Nor did I need anyone's permission or approval. You, Rick, and Evelyn made me feel empowered. You gave *me* control."

Rick added, "That reminds me of a statement from General George Patton. 'Tell a man exactly what needs to be done and let him surprise you with his ingenuity.' That's precisely what Kelly did. Except it didn't surprise any of us."

Addressing Kelly, Hal added, "Your visit with us, Kelly, *was* a surprise *and* a blessing, just like you! Thank you again for dropping in and sharing a few of your experiences with us. May I suggest we all say our goodbyes to Kelly and take a short break? The restrooms are just down the hall, if needed. We still have a lot to cover when we get back."

Soni spoke up, "Kelly, before you leave, I must ask. Was the young boy you rode bikes with named Danny?"

Kelly was shocked. "Yes, ma'am. But I didn't mention that. How on earth did you know his name?"

Soni smiled. "The universe has been speaking to me all week."

Section 7: HOW AND WHO

A Game Changer

Back to our topic at hand," Rick resumed. "Soni, another improvement to Rolly's ***Self*-Management Program** involves our tricycle and the role it plays in helping a person become *self*-managed. Please position our tricycle over the **What** Key on the display. To get to our discussion of the **How** and **Who** Keys, we must begin there."

Soni honored Rick's request. "I feel like a kid playing Monopoly. When do I get my two hundred dollars for passing Go?" she jokingly asked.

Rick smiled. "The payoff comes when your team manages to become *self*-managed. Everyone passes 'Go' *and* gets their money when that happens. We all win!"

"I'm liking this game more and more. Especially having a cool, little tricycle piece as opposed to a thimble or an iron."

"Your comment is highly fitting as you will soon move this tricycle piece around this new board."

"All the more intriguing!"

"Our intentions exactly. We also intend to keep it simple as we introduce five new documents to the program—and the tricycle is featured on documents three and four."

Soni removed her portfolio from her handbag and placed it on the table. "I can't wait. I'm ready for what all of you bring to the table, literally."

"Terrific! Let's begin with several questions: Have you ever found yourself in a situation where you were responsible for doing something vitally important, but didn't know what tasks were involved? . . . Where you were clueless regarding the requirements and expectations? . . . Where you had no way of knowing if you were anywhere close to competent in doing them? . . . And, where you were at a loss as to how you would ever become competent?"

Soni rolled her eyes. "Have I ever! You just described '**What** my current situation was' when I first got into sales before I attended Rolly's training. I was lost."

"You'll be pleased to know that the tools we're about to share will make certain that 'lost' feeling doesn't happen to any new people you bring on board or to any of your existing people. These documents will prove to be a game changer for you—and them."

"I like games. And I like change, especially when it's for the better."

"This is, Soni. By now, we expect you are well aware of the importance of the **What** Key and its Serving Man."

"More than ever," Soni responded. "But I've got a sneaky suspicion I'm about to learn a lot more about it."

"We're about to find out. The first three documents will focus on that Key." Rick looked across the table. "Hal, would you please share all five with Soni?"

Class Act

Gladly, Rick." Hal handed Soni the stack of pages he had placed at his seat during the break. She inserted them behind the tab she had prelabeled 'Phoenix Visit.' "Soni, before we delve into these, I'll refer back to Rick's comment about keeping this simple. The simplest way to understand how one person helps another become *self*-managed is to relate it to an experience we are all familiar with—our years of attending school. For our purpose, we'll concentrate on the four years of high school."

Soni sat up straight as if she were back in the classroom. "You've got my full attention, *Teacher* Looney."

Hal grinned. "Let's keep it that way, *Student* Soni. Now, let's get to the courses offered. In place of the traditional reading, writing, and arithmetic, our courses will equate to TASKS—things your team will be expected to know, or learn, and then be able to perform."

"TASKS instead of courses. I'm with you so far." Soni glanced at the title of the first document. "Is that what this TASK LIST page is for?"

"Yes, ma'am. And the second document, titled TASK REQUIREMENTS & EXPECTATIONS, specifies the details of what they're expected to know and do for each task on their list."

Soni flipped to that page. "I can see that, Hal."

"Once all their tasks have been identified, as well as what they're expected to know and do with each, we need a way to grade their proficiency—just like in school."

"We're talking a report card, right?" Soni asked.

"Right. If you'll turn to the third page, you'll discover something exciting about this document."

Doing so, Soni grinned when she saw the image of the tricycle front and center on the TASK REPORT CARD. "You're right, I'm super excited about this one!"

"Wait until you learn what it does, Soni. Just as a school report card gives us a *grade* for the course and a *score* for their conduct, ours does the same.

> "Then, the grade they receive for each task tells them which classroom they will be assigned to attend. The score tells them which row they'll be seated in."

Hal continued, "You'll notice these also relate to the fourth document."

Soni turned to that page. "This TASK CLASSROOM ASSIGNMENT looks most interesting, too, Hal. It also has a tricycle. Additionally, I see it identifies four classrooms: *Freshman, Sophomore, Junior,* and *Senior.* And each classroom is divided into distinct areas: a *Front Row,* a *Middle Row,* and a *Back Row* with each a different color. Oh, I see there's also an area described as the *Hall.* Is that anything like the 'principal's office'?"

Hal grinned. "Very observant, Soni. Yes, ma'am, being sent there could equate to being in the *Hall.* I'll have the privilege of addressing this page when the time comes."

"There's a lot going on in what I've seen of the first four, Hal, and I expect the fifth to follow suit. If these are the 'game changer' Rick says they are, I want to know how to play to win. Is it asking too much to go through these in great detail so I can understand the ins and outs of them completely?"

WHAT – TASK LIST

It's not asking too much at all, Soni. We expect nothing less. It's important you feel comfortable with them. I'll get started with document one." As Soni flipped back to the first page, Hal continued. "Our TASK LIST is where they identify the tasks they need to do. As you can see, it provides adequate space to list *all* the things they're responsible for knowing and doing. And there can be a lot."

"I see the wisdom in identifying and writing these down. That's the only way they, and we, can clearly recognize *everything* that needs to be done for their role. I imagine many of these can be found in their job description. May I ask what the three columns to the right, labeled 'Lowest CAPABILITY *Grade*' and 'Lowest WILLINGNESS *Score*' pertain to, as well as the 'Order of Attention Needed'?"

"Sure. The first two columns come from our TASK REPORT CARD, which Rick will address shortly. Once that information has been transferred, the last column of the TASK LIST allows the student and teacher to prioritize the order the tasks will be addressed. Why is that important? Because not all tasks are created equal. Some are more important than others, and both the student and teacher need to agree on which ones will take precedence. For now, let's examine the REQUIREMENTS and EXPECTATIONS associated with these tasks. This next document is Tiffany's favorite." Soni turned to document two.

WHAT – TASK REQUIREMENTS & EXPECTATIONS

Soni," Tiffany began, "as I reflect on *my* first year in new home sales, my discussions with Rolly regarding REQUIREMENTS and EXPECTATIONS were extremely beneficial. Remember that I had no back wheels on my tricycle. That meant my current situation at the **What** Key would have been 'blissful ignorance'—I didn't know what I didn't know."

Soni rolled her eyes and grinned. "Blissful ignorance. Been there, done that! Not to put you on the spot, but can you give me an example of an important task where specifying the REQUIREMENTS and EXPECTATIONS helped you?"

"Sure. The most rewarding was when Rolly and Rick helped me host a training event for Realtors at my model."

"Excuse me. Did you say training event? And at your model? Most salespeople will make a Realtor presentation at *their* office where they bring donuts or breakfast burritos, hand out brochures, talk about their neighborhood, and then invite them out to see it. With minimal success, I might add."

"You are correct. That old 'dog and pony show' *is* what most do. But that's not what *we* did. I'm sure you're familiar with the adage, 'Give a man a fish, and you feed him for a day. Teach him how to fish, and you feed him for a lifetime.' "

"I am. I've shared that with my teenagers."

"*We* wanted to do more than fill their bellies with food and their minds with information—all which was really to benefit *us* when you get down to it. Instead, we hoped to give them something of value that could help them every day in their lives and careers—something that would benefit *them*.

Our ultimate EXPECTATION was to add value to their lives and to hopefully gain their business long-term."

"That sounds like Rolly. You mentioned teaching them how to fish. By chance, does this involve Goldfish? I know he loves them," Soni playfully remarked.

Tiffany grinned. "That he does, but this does not. Because the training on DISC behavioral styles we received was so impactful—understanding how we and others see the world—we offered to teach that segment to entire brokerages at our models. On it, you specify the REQUIREMENTS of what you *know* needs to be done and then apply the *skills* you develop to do it."

"The back wheels of the tricycle."

"Exactly," Tiffany stated. "You will discover that these REQUIREMENTS often become the steps to follow to accomplish a task and will cover all the moves on your new 'Monopoly' board."

"I'm guessing it has been a while since you've been doing these, but can you recall and share the things you were required to do? It would help me better understand this."

"If Rick will serve as my wingman?" She got a thumbs-up from Rick. "I'll do them by number and describe them as I would have then. I'll also provide an explanation, if needed."

"That will be most helpful, Tiffany."

> "REQUIREMENT 1: Meet with Rolly to look at possible dates and set a budget. Confirm whether he or Rick will conduct the training."

"Rick was a part of this?" Soni asked.

"Yes, ma'am. I hadn't learned to teach DISC at that time. Rick had." Rick smiled.

> "REQUIREMENT 2: Identify potential brokerages to contact and begin making calls.
> REQUIREMENT 3: Confirm a brokerage and date, along with a preference for the type of food. Get a list of the number of agents attending. Order Behavioral Assessment packets. Select a vendor to provide chairs and tables.
> REQUIREMENT 4: Select a caterer to prepare the meal."

Soni interrupted, "Let me get this straight. You're providing training . . . a full meal . . . *and* in your models! You all went *all* out."

Rick interjected, "We wanted the word to *get* out to other brokerages about what we were doing. That news spread like wildfire. The next time around, we didn't have to do Requirement 2—to list potential brokerages to target and start calling. They were calling us."

"I would think so," Soni responded. "I'm impressed!"

Rick turned to address Tiffany. "I'm impressed with how this has stuck with you after all these years. I don't believe you need my help with the rest. You're almost halfway there." Tiffany gave Rick a thumbs-up this time.

Rick turned back to Soni. "Keep in mind that completing this list of REQUIREMENTS and EXPECTATIONS typically required six to seven weeks, with a timeline and deadlines."

Soni added, "This essentially provides a plan of **How** to make this task happen—our Fifth Key and Serving Man, along with our Sixth Key addressing **Who** will help and hold us accountable."

"That it is," Tiffany agreed. "So back to the numbers . . .

> REQUIREMENT 5: Meet with the marketing team to create and print invitations.
> REQUIREMENT 6: Send out invitations and notify our model cleanup crew of the date.
> REQUIREMENT 7: Confirm receipt of the invitations with the brokerage. Prepare neighborhood brochures and Behavioral Assessment packets for the Realtors.
> REQUIREMENT 8: Verify all is in order with Rolly, Rick, brokerage, caterer, vendor, and cleanup crew.
> REQUIREMENT 9: Set up the room. Welcome our guests. Conduct the training. Serve the meal."

Rick spoke up again, "If I might interject something here. We would always invite our salespeople from nearby communities to participate, especially in serving the food. It allowed them to speak to everyone and begin to develop a connection for future business, too."

"We all benefited that way. It was a 'we' experience," Tiffany added. "So, back to where we left off . . .

> REQUIREMENT 9 (*continued*): Enjoy the meal and fellowship. Clean up afterward.
> REQUIREMENT 10: Write and mail personal, handwritten thank-you cards. Make phone calls to invite Realtors back to bring the families they serve to see us. Schedule appointments. Write purchase agreements."

Tiffany paused for a moment. You could almost see the wheels turning in her mind. "I think that's everything," she added. "Whew!" Rick, Hal, and Soni gave Tiffany a standing ovation, pumping their fists in the air and exchanging high-fives before they sat back down.

Soni spoke up. "That was amazing! *You* are amazing!"

"Thank you, Soni. What's *really* amazing is the response we received from these brokerages. We became the builder of choice for these Realtors when they had families they were representing interested in a new home."

Hal added, "Plus, unlike our competition that had to offer hefty Realtor bonuses to attempt to *buy* their business, we did not. This minimal investment of time and money paid big dividends for the years the three of us were there. I participated in this after I joined the team. Definitely fun and fulfilling."

Tiffany interjected, "Hal's right. I think for all of us, the biggest payoff—the ultimate EXPECTATION of this task—was the difference we made in the lives *and* livelihood of these Realtors. We provided them with tools to help them improve their lives *and* careers. We became close friends with many."

"I can see that, Tiffany," Soni stated.

"Back to the relationships. After Rolly, Rick, and Hal moved on to other opportunities, I left new home sales and became a Realtor at one of these brokerages."

Rick interjected, "And not just *a* Realtor. She became *the* Realtor who won many awards! She rode that tricycle to the pinnacle of a second career. And is *still* riding it."

"I am not at all surprised," Soni admitted.

"You're too kind, Rick," Tiffany responded. "Speaking of tricycles, I believe it's time for you to address our TASK REPORT CARD."

Rick smiled. "That it is, Tiffany."

WHAT – TASK REPORT CARD

Flipping to document three, Soni grinned again when she saw the image of the tricycle near the upper-center portion of the page—the back wheels to the left, the front wheel facing right. A young boy was seated on the tricycle, his feet on the pedals and hands on the handlebars. The smile on his face matched Soni's.

She immediately noticed a dotted line dividing the back wheels from the front wheel and handlebars. One back wheel was labeled *KNOWLEDGE*, the other *SKILLS*, with the heading CAPABILITY above the two. Each back wheel could be graded with an A, B, C, or D.

In contrast, the front wheel was labeled *ATTITUDE*, and the handlebars marked *DIRECTION*. The heading WILLINGNESS was above both. Each of those could be scored with a 1, 2, 3, or 4.

Rick spoke up, "Soni, I cannot overstate the importance of this document. Without a way to grade the student's CAPABILITY with each task, as well as score their WILLINGNESS to perform it, the student and the teacher are essentially helpless—with no clear understanding of **What** their current situation is."

"I can appreciate that, Rick."

"While similarities exist between a school report card and this one, differences exist as well. One area where they differ is in the number of things they report on. A school report card lists several courses of study. This one will be for only *ONE* specific task."

"*One* report card *per* task. Got it," Soni confirmed.

"Good. Now, let's look at a similarity. As Hal mentioned, a school report card gives a grade for the course *and* a score for the student's conduct. Ours is similar—just a shift in mindset. The grade given for the CAPABILITY with each TASK equates to the classroom they're assigned to. You noted those earlier. A higher grade puts the student in a higher-level classroom. A lower grade means a lower-level classroom. As for the WILLINGNESS Score to perform the task, it equates to the row where they're seated. A score of 1 puts the student in the *Front Row*. A score of 4 in the *Hall*."

"So, who grades or scores what?"

"Good question, Soni. Here's how to determine one's CAPABILITY Grade: After the student and teacher identify everything the student must know *and* be able to do to perform the task—as outlined in the TASK REQUIREMENTS & EXPECTATIONS document—they both grade each back wheel. In the block provided, the student enters a grade of A, B, C, or D that they give themselves for the KNOWLEDGE they have acquired. The teacher does the same, entering the grade they give them in the adjoining box."

"I'm with you so far."

"Good. They do the same for the SKILLS boxes. Note that below the entered grades, the lowest grade determines which classroom the student will be assigned to attend. Hal will cover this in document four."

"I need to see how it all falls into place," Soni stated as she glanced at Hal. He gave her an affirmative nod.

"The same steps are taken to arrive at a WILLINGNESS Score. To clarify, the handlebars labeled *DIRECTION* determine if the student is clear on where they are going with the task. If not, are they willing to take direction? The second labeled *ATTITUDE* points to the front wheel—does the person possess the *want* to, the motivation, the desire, to tackle and complete the task? Are they eager to put forth the effort? The score of 1, 2, 3, and 4 beside each competency allows for evaluation, with 1 as the highest. As before, the student and teacher enter their score to determine where the student is seated in the classroom. Are they in the *Front, Middle*, or *Back Row*, or given a seat in the *Hall*?"

"Allow me to see if I get the essence of this document, Rick. Its purpose is to enable a teacher and student to ascertain an objective grade of the student's CAPABILITY regarding their *KNOWLEDGE* of what to do and their *SKILLS* of how to do it, as well as an objective score of their WILLINGNESS to take *DIRECTION* and their *ATTITUDE* about doing what needs to be done on a specific task. Is that it?"

Rick responded, "In a nutshell. You reach an *objective* grade and score as opposed to a *subjective* guess, or worse yet, no guess at all. This CAPABILITY Grade and WILLINGNESS Score are what get transferred to the TASK LIST document from earlier."

"Got it. Knowing these tools are the latest enhancements to the ***Self*-Management Program**, I'm guessing they were not around when the three of you were working with Rolly."

"Formally, no, ma'am. Informally, yes, ma'am. What I mean by that is the concepts were there and being applied. We identified the TASKS that needed to be done. We spelled out the REQUIREMENTS and EXPECTATIONS. We determined their CAPABILITY and WILLINGNESS to do them. And on the fourth document, we examined how we could assist them in mastering these tasks. We just didn't have these actual documents."

A Review

I can appreciate that, Rick. So, can you walk me through how these first three documents would have applied, had they been around then?"

"I'd be happy to, Soni. Let's take what we just talked about regarding Tiffany. We'll begin with the first document we discussed." Soni flipped back to that first page. " 'Hosting a DISC training event for Realtors at her model' would have been one of many tasks entered on her TASK LIST. And because of its importance, it would have been a priority."

"Yes, I also value its benefits."

"Focusing on that specific task, the ten REQUIREMENTS Tiffany just walked us through would have been entered on her TASK REQUIREMENTS & EXPECTATIONS document." Soni turned to that page. "EXPECTATIONS regarding timeframe and desired outcomes would also have been included."

"I see that." Soni flipped to the next page, document three. "Now we're to the TASK REPORT CARD. Walk me through it, please."

"Certainly, as long as *you* provide the answers. At that time, where would you rank Tiffany on the back wheels of her *KNOWLEDGE* and *SKILLS* regarding this task?"

Soni glanced at Tiffany. "No offense intended, but at the lowest CAPABILITY Grade, a D."

"None taken," Tiffany responded. "I would agree with that grade. I didn't know what I didn't know."

"I gave her a D, also," Rick confided. "That CAPABILITY Grade of D would assign her to the *Freshman Classroom D* that Hal is about to cover. Now to the front wheel of *ATTITUDE* and the handlebars of *DIRECTION*. Where would you score her on these?"

"I'd give her a WILLINGNESS Score of 1 on both. From what I've seen and heard, Tiffany has a positive attitude about everything and seems more than willing to take direction."

Tiffany smiled, "Thank you, Soni."

Rick responded, "And again, I agree with you, Soni. With a WILLINGNESS Score of 1, she would be seated in the *Front Row* of *Freshman Classroom A*. To help you visualize what this looks like, it's time for Hal to walk us through the TASK CLASSROOM ASSIGNMENT document." Soni turned to it.

HOW AND **WHO** – TASK CLASSROOM ASSIGNMENT

"Soni," Hal responded, "this document brings us to the **How** and **Who** Keys and their Serving Men. You might position your tricycle between these two Keys on our laminated display. The document shows the four classrooms: *Freshman D,* at the lower left, *Senior A,* at the upper right, and *Sophomore C* and *Junior B,* separating those. Are you with me so far?"

"I am."

"You noticed earlier that the floor of each classroom is divided into colored rows: the *Front Row* is green, the *Middle Row* yellow, the *Back Row* red, and the *Hall* black."

"So, let me guess how this works," Soni requested. "If we enter Tiffany's CAPABILITY Grade of D and her WILLINGNESS Score of 1, this would put her in the *Front Row* of *Freshman Classroom D*. Is that correct?"

"It is." Soni moved the tricycle from the display to this location on the document. "Now, what will Rolly's *Role* and *Tone* be in her mirror?"

"All the possible *Roles,* as listed above the classrooms, indicate how he would address her level of CAPABILITY," Soni replied. "The answer provided above Freshman Classroom D indicates he would take on a *DIRECTIVE Role*. All his possible *Tones,* as listed at the end of the rows, indicate how he would address her level of WILLINGNESS. The answer at the end of the green row says to present a *Congratulatory Tone*. This makes sense. She's new, so she needs someone directing her actions, for her benefit and with her permission. *And* she needs to feel good about where she is."

"Spot on. Now let's bring in our **Where** Key and Serving Man into this discussion. Where would Tiffany and Rolly want her to be on this page?"

"That's easy. On her tricycle in the *Front Row* of *Senior Classroom A*," Soni answered, moving the tricycle to that space. "There, his *Role* is to *EMPOWER* her and still *Congratulate* her for being in that *Front Row*."

"You got it, Soni. Just so we're clear on the teacher's *Role* in each classroom, walk me through their *Role* as the student progresses from *Freshman,* to *Sophomore,* to *Junior,* to *Senior*."

"The teacher's *Role* transitions from *DIRECTING,* to *GUIDING,* to *COUNSELING,* to *EMPOWERING*."

"Excellent. Now let's shift to their need to *Be Present* in the classroom."

"Sure. It goes from *VERY OFTEN,* to *QUITE OFTEN,* to *OFTEN,* to *NOT OFTEN.*"

"So far, so good. And their level of *Involvement* with the student?"

"From *IMMENSE,* to a *GOOD BIT,* to *SOME,* to *MINIMAL.*"

"And lastly, the amount of *Time* they would expect to spend with them on this task?"

"From a *GREAT DEAL,* to a *GOOD DEAL,* to *NOT MUCH,* to the *LEAST.*" Soni took a moment to ponder all these answers. "Is there a reason all these are left so undefined? A percentage isn't given or a number? Perhaps a ranking?"

"Great question, Soni. So many extenuating circumstances exist—travel time to get to that student, the number of students they're responsible for, even the student's DISC behavioral style: Eagle, Parrot, Dove, or Owl as taught in **S.M.I.L.E.** These could all come into play. So, we felt it best to empower the teacher to make that decision of how to interpret their meaning best. Does that make sense?"

"If we're trying to practice what we preach, it does. They *should* be empowered to make that call."

"That takes care of each classroom. Now let's conclude with their *Tone* with the student."

"That's easy, Hal. The *Tone* doesn't change from classroom to classroom. If they're seated in the *Front Row*, the teacher will always assume a *Congratulatory Tone.*"

"That's a place of celebration. We want them to feel good about their *DIRECTION* and *ATTITUDE*. Please continue."

"If they're seated in the *Middle Row*, the teacher will *Cheer* them on—hoping to get them to that *Front Row*."

"Correct. Their *DIRECTION* and *ATTITUDE* are acceptable, although not where they need them to be. One would expect they'll have a conversation about what's going on that's put them in that row. What about the *Back Row*?"

"If they're seated there, the teacher will *CONFRONT* them? Does that mean they'll be in their face?"

"Yes, ma'am. Respectfully, but yes, ma'am. Please note this is their WILLINGNESS Score. It's about their behavior, *not* who they are. There's a difference. Who they are is about the values and principles of the person on the seat of their tricycle. How they behave is what we observe in their *ATTITUDE* and *DIRECTION*. A lack of eagerness, enthusiasm, or effort might be another way of looking at it. Along with reluctance or aversion to take *DIRECTION*."

"This is making so much sense, Hal. And what if they don't like that *CONFRONTATION*?"

"Tough. We are there to help and/or hold them accountable. And the *only* reason we are in their mirrors is because they either requested it *or* gave us permission to be there. Let's go back to your visit to Ester and Rob's gym. You represent the training partner who ensures the member shows up and *does* what they've agreed to do. You have agreed to hold them accountable. Which means you're doing what *you* agreed to do. You with me?"

"Yes, sir. That helped, Hal. Thanks. So, what about the *Hall* position? That sounds pretty serious. Is this where I get the answer to my earlier question?"

"It is, Soni. And thank you for your patience. It means they have been removed from the classroom because their negative attitude not only is *affecting* them, but also has the potential to *infect* the others on the team."

"Unfortunately, I've seen that happen, Hal."

"We all have, Soni. One rotten apple can spoil the bunch. And very quickly, I might add."

"I can't help but think back to my conversation with Karen and Vicky. Is it possible a person's negative attitude could be a result of something they are struggling with?"

"It's very possible. And if that's the case, we do our best to help them work through whatever it is. That's where love and trust come in."

"That's good to know. But what if it's not about struggles? What if it's . . . well . . . just them? Some people are just wired that way."

"Then we will likely have a 'come to Jesus' meeting. If they can turn it around? Great. If they can't, you have the answer for that, don't you?"

"Yes, sir," Soni responded with a shrug. "They may be encouraged to take their excellence elsewhere."

"Sometimes the best way to change a person, is to change a person."

"Oh, I've got to remember that. Let's go back to those we *can* help. Can I assume it's not necessary for someone in *Freshman Classroom D* to have to graduate to the *Sophomore* and then *Junior* class, before moving to a *Senior* class?"

"You're correct. Let's go back to Tiffany's example. If, after her experience in *Freshman Classroom D*, she were to demonstrate she could perform this task the next time at an A CAPABILITY Grade and 1 WILLINGNESS Score, she would skip the other classrooms and take a position in the *Front Row* of *Senior Classroom A*."

"It's comforting to know that if she were doing senior-level work, she would be in a senior class."

"As she should. She would have demonstrated the ability to become *self*-managed in *that* task and would no longer need us in her mirror. She would be empowered. Our goal would be the same as hers—that she gets there with *every task*. With some tasks, she may need help. With others, she may not. These tools help us determine that, as well as how to get her there."

"Speaking of us in their mirrors, before we move to the final document, I'm curious why the italicized words, *'if needed,'* are beside the field in the heading for the teacher's name on each of these documents? Does that imply it could be left blank?"

"It does, Soni. The only time a name would appear in this space is when the student has *requested,* or *given permission,* for someone to be there. To clarify, *any* reference to a teacher in the discussions the four of us have is not meant to imply a teacher will necessarily be involved. We four—all being *self*-managed individuals—know full well that much, if not all, of this can be done without someone else to help or hold us accountable. Are you with us on this?"

"Yes, sir. What you're saying is that if we referred to a teacher in our discussion, that doesn't mean a teacher would necessarily be needed."

"That's it, Soni. So, back to your question. If that field is blank, the student considers themself to be *self*-managed with that specific task—thus no teacher is needed."

"So, this space could be viewed as the mirror on either *or* both walls behind the double doors opened by our Sixth Serving Man, **Who**. Is that correct?"

"Yes, ma'am, Soni. Ester and Rob schooled you well."

"The time with them at their gym will stick with me forever. During that visit, I understood that the person in the mirror could be anyone. Is that the case here?"

"Absolutely. It doesn't have to be someone they report to. Oftentimes, it's another salesperson on their team. During our years together, the three of us filled that role many times, as did others on our team." Rick and Tiffany nodded in agreement.

"Now I know why you were so excited to share these." Soni moved the tricycle aside and turned to the last page. "Who's going to help me with the EMPOWERMENT REVIEW SESSIONS?" she asked. "This looks pretty darn important!"

Tiffany responded, "It is, Soni . . . big time important! We agreed to share this one among us. If it's okay with these gentlemen, I'll begin." Hal and Rick nodded their approval.

EMPOWERMENT REVIEW SESSIONS

Antiquated versions of this document have been around forever, Soni. The name 'Planned Encounter' was often used to describe them—a name I never really cared for."

Rick interjected, "I certainly didn't. The name took me back to the ant hill that reminded me of the movie I mentioned. To this day, it makes my skin crawl just thinking about it!"

Hal read the definition he pulled up on his phone. "*Encounter: To meet as an adversary or enemy.* Not very pretty. The fact that these encounters were *planned* makes it even worse. It sets a rather unpleasant tone."

"I'm also familiar with the name, and never cared for it either," Soni admitted. "But EMPOWERMENT REVIEW SESSIONS? Well, that sounds more user-friendly."

Tiffany added, "And when you look at what's in it, I believe you'll agree with that even more. The old 'Planned Encounter' felt more like an '*I got you*' event. This feels like a '*How can I help you?*' experience."

"I agree," Rick stated. "On the left side of the page, you'll notice five categories listed from top to bottom:

- GOAL VS. NET SALES
- DANCE TO S.M.I.L.E.
- RUN THE BUSINESS
- MAINTAIN BUSINESS
- QUALITY OF LIFE

"Soni, as you can see, specific details are broken down to the right of each of these. We'll touch on a few as we discuss each category. Also, please note that this document was created specifically for new home sales. It can be customized for *any* discipline, in *any* industry."

"That's such an important clarification," Soni remarked, "Thank you!"

Hal spoke up. "Across the top of the page, from left to right, you see the year is broken down into quarters, with the possibility of two sessions per month below each. The actual scores to enter in the fields under each session are shown in the legend. And the average of the scores and ratings are shown quarter by quarter and year to date throughout the year."

"This seems to bring together much of what a business plan addresses," Soni stated.

"That's pretty much it," Tiffany agreed, "with a different name. Candidly, we toyed with calling it that but longed for something more in tune with what becoming *self*-managed represents. When we learned of Karen's 'in-the-shower' inspiration, we knew we had our answer. EMPOWERMENT REVIEW SESSIONS says it all. She made it easy for us."

"That she did," Soni smiled.

Rick spoke up, "Back to the five categories, Soni. To the right of GOAL VS. NET SALES, you'll notice we've identified the different sources of sales. We combined Karen and Vicky's terms of PILLARS with Craig's SOI to describe them."

"I like that," Soni remarked. "What are the two images to the right that appear to be gauges?"

Hal replied, "There's that 'attention to detail' again," making Soni grin. "We'll get to that shortly. For now," he said, "let's discuss the DANCE TO S.M.I.L.E. category, Soni."

"I recognize the four colored dance floors Rolly teaches that represent the sales experience the salesperson creates with their 'dance partners'—their guests," she noted.

"And the five essential elements of **S.M.I.L.E.** are integrated into that experience," Hal added.

"That would make sense. They're one in the same. I see it provides the opportunity to track their proficiency using the DANCE REVIEW Cards provided during the sales training."

"That's a big part of this category, Soni. In addition, their effectiveness in using their Guest *'I Care'* Stay-in-Touch

Program and Ambassador Club *'I Still Care'* Stay-in-Touch Program is also scored. If we're doing okay thus far, I'll ask Tiffany to address the RUN THE BUSINESS category."

"I'm doing more than fine. Please continue."

"Your wish is my command," Tiffany smiled. "This category addresses how they operate their business. Rolly taught us to see ourselves as actually running our own business. Let's touch on a few areas of importance":

- ❑ *Accurate Paperwork*
- ❑ *Profitability—Selling Within Pricing Parameters*
- ❑ *Manage Homebuyer Expectations*
- ❑ *Eliminate Mistakes/Concessions*
- ❑ *Co-Manage Neighborhood with Builder*
- ❑ *Monitor Loan Approval and Escrow Process*
- ❑ *Monitor Status of Contingencies*
- ❑ *Homeowner Satisfaction Rating*
- ❑ *In-House Mortgage Capture Ratio*

"Wow—all critical areas," Soni acknowledged. "Rick mentioned this document can be customized. I take it I could add additional fields to this if desired?"

"Absolutely. You can change anything, anywhere. *Your* wish is at *your* command."

"I like that even more, Tiffany. Again, I notice two more images to the right that appear to be gauges. Is this the time to address these as well as the other two?"

"Not yet, but we'll get there shortly," Rick responded with a grin. "Let's address the MAINTAIN BUSINESS category. As you can see, these are fairly straightforward":

- ❑ *Website Information Accurate and Up-to-Date*
- ❑ *Files and Sales/Marketing Materials Organized*
- ❑ *Refreshments Stocked*
- ❑ *Model Condition/Landscaping*
- ❑ *Available Homes Condition*
- ❑ *Neighborhood Cleanliness*
- ❑ *Signage/Flags/Landscaping*

"The routine things that often get overlooked," Soni affirmed. "Correct me if I'm wrong, but you could find these tasks on the TASK LIST."

"You've been paying attention, Soni. Yes, ma'am, they would appear on that list. Let's move on to the last category of QUALITY OF LIFE. Hal, are you up for this one?"

Hal smiled. "More than ready. During our conversation with Karen and Vicky regarding STRUGGLES, we were moved by the caring message they conveyed. So much so, we included the following":

- ❑ *Family/Relationships*
- ❑ *Self/Health*
- ❑ *Spirituality*
- ❑ *Wealth Creation/Money*
- ❑ *Non-Negotiables*

"I was moved by the power of these as well, Hal."

"You'll also notice we included the topic of NON-NEGOTIABLES."

"I'm pleased to see that. This category is a reminder of the words Vicky shared that resonated with me. She stated we should not view 'successful business' and 'quality of life' as being an 'either-or' proposition. Instead, we should see it as a 'both-and' opportunity."

Hal paused to reflect on Vicky's words. "A paradigm of *inclusion*, not *exclusion*. A beautiful way to see the world."

"So true. Speaking of seeing, this time I see a yellow circle to the right that resembles a light. If everyone intended to pique my interest by waiting to discuss the gauges and light, mission accomplished. Is this the time to address these?"

The Dashboard

"We thought you'd never ask, Soni." Hal's droll remark drew a smirk from Soni, followed by her smile and a playful slap on his wrist. Hal laughed and turned to his left. "Tiffany has agreed to speak to these."

"Thank you, Hal. Adhering to the idea of *keeping it simple*—the ***S*** in **S.M.I.L.E.**—the three of us looked for a way to simplify everything you've received."

"That's helpful, Tiffany. On this page alone, I counted more than thirty-some-odd areas to consider."

"Being familiar with *all* the documents in the ***Self-*Management Program**, we identified five gauges that can tell us whether everything is working properly or not."

"You mean like gauges on a car?"

"Exactly. Let me explain. Before I began my drive this morning, after starting my engine, I checked the *Battery Gauge* on my dashboard to see if the battery was charging. Without electricity to power all the systems, I wouldn't be able to go anywhere. Next, I glanced at the *Oil Pressure Gauge.* If the oil is not lubricating the engine, everything will go up in smoke—

literally! The *Temperature Gauge* was next. For maximum efficiency, the coolant in the engine must operate within a safe temperature range. Not too cold. Not too hot. By the way, my stepfather taught me all this stuff."

"He did a good job, Tiffany. Thankfully, mine did, too."

"Good for him, and good for you, Soni. Then I checked my *Fuel Gauge.* I've learned the hard way that I kinda need fuel in the tank to get me where I want to be."

"I've overlooked that little detail more than once. I'm not happy when that happens."

"Who is, Soni? Once these checked out, I began my journey. Every so often, I would glance at the gauges on my dashboard to make certain everything was still okay."

"What about the fifth gauge you mentioned?"

"The fifth gauge is a *Warning Light* controlled by my car's computer. If I drift from my lane, or have been driving too long without a break, my *Driver Warning Light* will glow, indicating I need to take a break—to pull over and stretch my legs."

"I *love* this!" Soni exclaimed. "Can you take me through how these five work on our journey to help our people get where they want to be, to become *self*-managed?"

Rick answered, "I was nominated earlier to take the lead on these, Soni. Let's begin with the GOAL VS NET SALES TOTALS Gauge. If a salesperson is meeting or exceeding their sales goals here, it's often a good indication something is going right."

"We hope that's the case most of the time. But we all know good sales numbers can also result from prices too low to begin with, or negotiating on price to make the sales happen."

"Which is why we look at another gauge on our dashboard—the Profitability Gauge. Are they selling within pricing parameters? These refer to the full price and do not exceed any incentive package that may be offered. If so, that's another positive indication something is going right."

"That's a *big* one, Rick. So, what's next?"

"Another *big* one, Soni. We look at our Homeowner (Customer) Satisfaction Gauge. If they're receiving stellar scores and getting a 'yes' to our question of whether they would recommend or refer us, something is going right again."

"That would tell me a *lot* of things are going right," Soni concluded. "Under the RUN THE BUSINESS category, the salesperson must be doing a great job of *Managing Homebuyer Expectations.*"

"You've got it, Soni. Great surveys are not always an indication that we've done everything right."

"I agree, Rick. Much of the time, it simply means they've prepared their buyers for the speed bumps they are likely to encounter along the way. No one likes surprises. Homeowners can be very forgiving when they trust us."

"That they can, Soni. Now, if they like us, if they trust us, if we've exceeded their expectations, and if we've stayed in touch with them during and after closing, continuing to show how much we care, we've earned the right to ask for and receive the 'Quality Introductions' we learned about from John Norris that result in referral sales. Which means our sales at the Referral PILLAR Gauge show all is well."

"These four gauges are all associated with business. I take it the *Driver's Warning Light* will address the personal side?"

"Very observant, Soni. If they're able to blend 'success in their career' with 'quality of life'—the items listed in that category—this warning light will never come on. This indicates they're experiencing the best of both worlds: an abundance of eggs *and* a healthy goose. *Aesop's Fable.* Production *and* production capability."

Road Service

"This is just toooo cooool! But, what happens if we, or they, see a concern with any of the gauges or the warning light along the way?" Soni inquired. Rick pointed to Hal and smiled.

Hal smiled back. "I believe it's my turn, Soni. If we see a concern, it's time they pull over. It's time to examine what might be causing the issue. If *they* request our help, we accept their invitation to visit them. If *we* initiate the conversation, they permit us to stop by. Either way, the tools that got them this far are used to analyze and fix what's not working properly so they can get back on the road."

"That makes perfect sense. While visiting with Karen and Vicky, they discussed the possibility of resetting sales goals if they're not being met. I can see that as an option when they're self-employed, like the women in their tribe. What are your thoughts when they're employed, like with your situation, Hal?"

"Well, when they're encouraged to set *their* goals first, they're likely to set them higher than the company's goals. I know that almost always happens with our team. If so, lowering them as Karen and Vicky discussed might work well as long as the company's goals are being met."

"I agree. But what if they're not?"

"Then we look at other factors. Are they properly executing all relevant tasks? Utilizing their PILLARS? Performing the vital steps in their DANCE that create value in themselves *and* their product, putting lots of smiles on lots of faces? Following their *'I Care'* Stay-in-Touch Program? The same applies to their *'I Still Care'* Stay-in-Touch Program for their Ambassadors. We'll also look at the market to see if anything has changed."

Soni shook her head. "It's *always* changing . . . *always* adjusting. If I had had these tools when our market changed, we wouldn't have had to shop our people. We would have already known those who were not performing well were not applying what they were taught from **S.M.I.L.E.** The ***Self*-Management Model** and these tools would have helped us help them meet or exceed their goals. We wouldn't have had to manage them. We could have helped them *self*-manage themselves. A missed *opportunity*!"

Hal smiled. "That's what the ***Self*-Management Model** and all these incredible tools are designed to do, Soni."

Soni picked up the tricycle and began moving it around the ***Self*-Management Model** display. "It appears we'll be visiting some, if not all, of these Keys to *self*-management and their Serving Men while doing so. Am I correct?"

"That you are, Soni. The model is not a one-and-done experience. The Six Keys and their Serving Men are always there for us and ready to help at any time needed."

Keep on Truckin'

It would seem so, Hal. Now, let's look at the other side of the coin. What happens when, month after month, and quarter after quarter, *all* the gauges are good? If *sales numbers, profitability, homeowner satisfaction,* and *referral sales* indicate everything is where it needs to be? And if no warning light is flashing, which tells us they're enjoying a *high quality of life,* does this tell us we can leave them alone?"

"I'd like to think it tells us we *must* leave them alone, Soni! It tells us we're no longer needed in their mirrors. They're on their tricycle in the *Front Row* of the *Senior Classroom A,* having mastered the things that matter most. Our dashboard provides a simple way to pay attention to the most important things."

Soni interjected, "It would tell us we have helped them grow a successful business without sacrificing their quality of life—Karen's purpose."

"Our purpose, too. And at the end of the year, we, and they, celebrate their successes, reset everything for the new year, and start over. To play off Tiffany's example, we plan another trip."

Tiffany spoke up, "I think it's time *I* made a trip to the ladies' room. My *Driver's Warning Light* just started flashing, telling me it's time for me to pull over and take a break."

"I expect we all could use another one," Hal remarked. Soni and Rick nodded in agreement.

Soni interrupted, "Before we do, I have a request." Referencing the page titled EMPOWERMENT REVIEW SESSIONS, she continued, "Since this is the last document, I'd like to have a few minutes to look over *all* the documents I've received this week and organize them *and* my thoughts on how I see applying them. Afterward, I'd like the three of you to help me fine-tune them for this journey I'll soon take with my team."

"I think that would be time well spent, Soni. It would be our pleasure to help you." Rick and Tiffany nodded. "How do you see going about this? What do you need from us?"

"Thanks for asking. I'm both visual *and* hands-on. In my office, I have a large wall covered with dry-erase boards. When I have a big project, I tape everything on the wall so I can see what I'm working with. Then, I begin moving things around until it comes together. It's just me . . . and the wall."

"I don't have a wall with dry-erase boards," Hal answered. "But I do have a large ballroom just across the hall where we hold our events. I can place folding tables end to end that might serve the same purpose."

"That would be perfect. I just need a way to view everything."

"I take it you'd like it to be just you and the tables—you and your wall—for the next little bit?"

"If that's okay? I work better that way. I shouldn't need more than thirty minutes."

Rick checked his watch. "That works perfectly for us all. I received word that another old friend of ours might stop by this afternoon for a visit. Why don't you take your break first, while Tiffany and I help Hal set up the tables? Then, we'll take our break, and we can connect with our friend. Does that work for everybody?" All nodded in agreement while Rick hid a sly grin on his face.

Section 8: A MEETING OF THE MINDS

From Top to Bottom

Soni found the ballroom dimly lit, with the floor arranged with chairs for an upcoming event. The stage, however, was bright. *I'm guessing that's where I'm supposed to be*, she assumed. As she made her way onto the stage, she saw four eight-foot tables had been placed end to end close to the front edge, facing the auditorium. At center stage stood a large, round table with the laminated display of the ***Self*-Management Model of Empowerment** and the tricycle placed upon it. She smiled when she noticed a fresh glass of her favorite tea, along with napkins, a box of tissues, sheets of blank paper, and a black marker—all on the table—plus a small bowl of Goldfish crackers. One of Hal's business cards sat there as well, with a note requesting she call when she finished. *These three are over the top with their level of service,* she thought as she took a sip of tea. *I'm impressed. If I want to impress them, I'd best get busy!*

She placed her portfolio on the round table and opened her first tab to remove the images she'd received from Ester and Rob. She spread them along the top of the first long table in the order she'd received them. She did the same at the second table for the documents from Karen and Vicky. She repeated that process from her third and fourth visits on the remaining two tables.

Where do I begin? she pondered the possibilities. *Since I received them in a logical order that follows the Six Keys, I should be able to keep most of them at the tables where they are and only have to move a few around. Let's see how this goes.*

Recalling the inspiration she drew from Karen and Vicky's website, she took a blank page from the round table. With the marker, she wrote **Blend** in bold letters, followed by a modified version of the *"What We Do"* message that she tailored to fit her situation.

Helping my team attain Success in Business without sacrificing their Quality of Life.

I love the tone this sets. It says I care about them and their success. And I do! They deserve the highest ROTI *on whatever investment of time they devote to their business. I want the best for them. And I should expect the best from them.* She proudly placed that page at the lower left corner of the first long table.

Expecting the best from them is about excellence! And that declaration told her what would follow. On another blank page, she wrote **Create a Culture of Excellence!** *That's the first message Rolly shared with his team. It set the standard for what was to come.* She placed that page beside the first. *It's where we must strive to be, both as individuals and as a team.*

What should follow this? She walked the tables perusing the documents, stopping when she got to the SIX PERSONAL PERSPECTIVES document at the third table. *These six points dovetail nicely into excellence.* She picked up this page and placed it next in line at the first table.

I also love the second thing Rolly did. He emphasized that he had worked with them. On another page, she wrote **Work With Them!** Before the ink could dry, Soni marked through that statement, flipped the page over, and wrote ***Play* With Them!** *The **E** in* **S.M.I.L.E.** *reminds me of the importance of seeing it as play and not work. This experience has to be enjoyable. It has to be fun! And using the word "With" sends the message it's something we will do together!* She placed that page next in line.

What follows? As she surveyed the documents on the second table, she noticed the definition of Empowerment that Karen and Vicky gave her. *I told them I wanted it among the first things I shared. My people must know I will empower them to be strong and more confident, especially in taking control of their lives and claiming their rights.* She placed it next in line.

Recalling that the ***Self*-Management Model of Empowerment** appeared on the back, she flipped it over. *They must know my ultimate goal is to help them become self-managed. Anything short of that proves unacceptable!* She turned the page back over and then moved the laminated display of the ***Self*-Management Model of Empowerment** from the round table and placed it next in line. Due to the size of this display, only two more documents could fit on the bottom row of table number one.

Staring at the Keys and doors on the laminated display, she knew what she wanted next. *The images of the Six Keys, so eye-catching on this model, is the perfect place to introduce Rudyard Kipling's poem.* She removed that page from the top row and placed the poem next in line on the bottom row. *They need to know that these Six Serving Men go to work for us every day—we just must be wise enough to take advantage of the help they offer with the Keys they hold.*

From here, the Image of the **What** Key *should follow.* She repositioned it on the bottom row beside the poem. That completed that row of the first table. She followed this process for the balance of the images and documents on the remaining tables. The order was as follows . . .

- **WHAT** IS MY SITUATION NOW?
- PAST-YEAR BUSINESS REVIEW
- PILLARS
- MAINTENANCE
- FOUR LAWS OF A DATABASE
- STRUGGLES
- TASK LIST
- TASK REQUIREMENTS & EXPECTATIONS
- TASK REPORT CARD

Image of the **Where** Key

- **WHERE** DO I WANT TO BE AND **WHEN?**
- LIFE GOALS
- CAST YOUR VISION
- NON-NEGOTIABLES

Image of the **Why** Key

- YOUR BIG LIFE
- YOUR VALUE PROPOSITION

Image of the **When** Key

- GOALS FOR REALISTIC ACHIEVERS
- GOALS FOR BIG DREAMERS

Image of the **How** Key

Image of the **Who** Key

- TASK CLASSROOM ASSIGNMENT
- CHOOSE AN ACCOUNTABILITY PARTNER
- EMPOWERMENT REVIEW SESSIONS

That takes care of them all. Soni took one last look at the order of everything laid out, methodically moving from page to page, pausing occasionally to reflect. *I need to add one more thing,* she thought, returning to the round table. Taking her marker and another blank page, she wrote **Hall of Fame**. *I love what Cheri did by posting everyone's performance on the walls. I cannot think of a better way to display their excellence!* She added this page to the last table.

Soni surveyed her work. *I like the rhyme and reason behind all of this. The way it all comes together makes total sense. And, best of all, everyone who has shared these documents with me has proven they work. All I have to do is follow their example, and my people will also become self-managed.*

She retrieved her phone from her handbag and took a video of each table. Just as she was about to dial Hal's number, the doors at the far end of the ballroom opened. "Is it okay if we come in?" Hal shouted. "We're anxious to see what you've done."

"Yes, sir," Soni replied as she put her phone away. "Your timing is perfect. I was about to call you."

With all on stage, the three took their time to examine the tables as they walked back and forth from one, to the other, to the other. Rick spoke first. "You've been busy, Soni. What you've done looks great."

Tiffany interjected, "I like what I see. Well done."

Hal spoke up, "For what it's worth, Soni, you've got my blessing."

"I thank all of you. I'm relieved to see this meets with everyone's approval. However, I did expect comments, or at least questions, regarding the pages I added at the beginning, as well as the one at the end."

"Oh, those are forthcoming," Rick assured her as he walked back to the first table. Everyone followed.

"Just not from us," Hal responded with a smirk.

"Yeah," Tiffany added. "We thought it wise to fly in someone far more qualified to give you that input."

Soni looked confused. Then astonished. She heard the sound of wings flapping, then *whoooosh!* Rolly flew to the stage, landing on the table in front of them. She was . . . stunned. "What on earth are you doing here?" she asked, extending her arms to give him a Texas-sized hug. "You said nothing on our phone call last night that indicated you would be coming here. What happened?"

"I reconnected with a close friend, David Osborn, at dinner Tuesday evening. He's the *New York Times* best-selling author of *Wealth Can't Wait*, the founder of Gobundance (a group of high-caliber professionals helping each other grow), and a widely respected real estate investor and entrepreneur—who also happens to own several Keller Williams franchises. He endorsed **S.M.I.L.E.**, which is how we met. David has a private jet and, much to my good fortune, mentioned he was flying to Phoenix this morning on business and offered for me to tag along. We will be returning to Austin with him tomorrow afternoon. When I say 'we,' I mean myself *and* you."

"This is too much," Soni exclaimed. "Following an invigorating workout this morning, I enjoyed a relaxing spa treatment, compliments of Cheri and Craig. This afternoon I get a ride in a limo, and I wrap up tomorrow afternoon with a flight on a private jet." She glanced at Hal. "I could get used to this *royalty* thing." Hal nodded and smiled.

"Well, Soni, it's not *that* private of a jet," Rolly confessed. "I've got two new friends and one old friend returning with us tomorrow."

"That's fine, Rolly. Any friend of yours is a friend of mine."

"Truer words have never been spoken. I believe the gentleman's name is . . . let me see . . . it's Todd."

"That will be easy to remember. *I* have a Todd."

"And he has two teenagers traveling with him."

"What a coincidence. Todd and I have two."

Rolly smiled. "I'm trying to recall their names. Give me a moment. I think the daughter is Abbey . . . Ashley . . . No. It's Ashton. That's it, Ashton. And the son's name is . . . "

"If you say Jaxon, I'm going to scream." Rolly covered his ears with his wings and smiled. The others did likewise. "You've got to be kidding me. It *is* Jaxon, isn't it!" she exclaimed at the top of her lungs. "My entire family is here?"

Rolly spread his wings as he gestured to the others. "We all decided to make it a family affair."

Soni was in shock. "How did you reach Todd, and where is everyone now?"

"LinkedIn. He was easy to find. We've been working on this since my dinner with David. Your family drove up last night to stay with me. As for where they are now, they're enjoying a round of golf at this magnificent course."

"You little stinker!" Soni responded by giving Rolly a bear hug. When do I get to see them?"

Hal interjected, "We just checked on them, Soni. They should finish in about forty-five minutes. I anticipate we'll wrap up about the same time."

Soni gave Hal a big hug. "You told me you wanted me to feel like royalty. You've outdone yourself big time."

"You can thank Rick and Tiffany for this, too. We've all been in on it. We know this week has been special, and we wanted it to end on a high note." Soni immediately gave Rick and Tiffany a hug.

"It *has* been. More than all of you can possibly imagine," Soni responded. She turned to address Rolly. "You never cease to amaze me, my friend. How can I ever thank you?"

Rolly pointed to the documents on the tables. "How about allowing me to look at what you've created here. May I?"

"I'd be honored. May I get you some Goldfish to snack on while you're doing so?" she asked, then smiled at Rick and shook her finger. "I totally missed the clue that an 'old friend of ours' might stop by for a visit." Rick shook his finger back and smiled.

Rolly snickered. "You've got to be on your toes around this bunch. Perhaps later with the Goldfish, Soni. Thanks."

A Common Thread

Rolly slowly walked from table to table, reviewing each page and document. Returning to the first table, he remarked, "All the documents are right where they should be, which tells me you have a keen understanding of how all this is designed to work."

Soni looked at Hal, Rick, and Tiffany and smiled. "I've had great teachers all week—present company included. Everyone has made it easy for me. They made me feel empowered to take ownership of what they gave me."

"This entire week was all about empowerment, Soni. I appreciate that you placed its definition alongside the image of the ***Self*-Management Model of Empowerment**, near the beginning. Wise move. If you don't mind, I'd like to get your explanation for the three handwritten pages you've included that precede them, as well as the last one."

"Gladly. Before I discuss the first three, allow me to share their overriding purpose, including the definition of empowerment, as the four are connected." Soni took a moment to gather her thoughts, searching for just the right words. "I noticed a common thread woven through my four visits. That thread is *love.* I believe it's the underlying reason for *their* success *and* the success of their people. And I'm convinced their people know it and feel it."

"I'm thankful you recognized that. I'm sure your people will, too." The others nodded in agreement.

"The same could be said for Vince Lombardi, whom Robin told me about during my Virginia visit. His legacy told us we *must* love our people. That love is *loyalty*. Love is *teamwork*. Love respects the *dignity* of the individual, and that *heart power* will be the strength of our team." Again, she paused—this time to regain her composure. "I love my people. I love what I do. And I want that love to be known *and* felt up front."

"I cannot think of a better mindset to begin this journey with your team," Rolly confessed.

"Thank you, sir." She pointed to the first page. "When I begin with **Blend**, it introduces the personalized version of Karen and Vicky's '*What We Do'*—of helping them attain success in business without sacrificing their quality of life. It's where *they* began. It *is* a blend. It promotes a '*both-and'* paradigm. Unlike the old farmer in that special *Aesop's Fable*, I promise to look out for the health of the goose, as well as the eggs it can produce. My people need to know and feel that, too."

"You've set a powerful tone beginning with this."

"Thank you, sir." Soni pointed to the next page. "Because I want the best *for* them, I should expect the best *from* them. This message is intended to convey the desire to **Create a Culture of Excellence!** I love how you set that expectation up front with your team in Dallas."

Rick interjected, "Rolly shared a quote during that first meeting I failed to mention earlier. Aristotle penned it somewhere around 350 B.C. I just pulled it up on my phone. 'Excellence is never an accident,' he wrote. 'It is always the result of high intention, sincere effort, and intelligent execution. It represents the wise choice of many alternatives. Choice, not chance, determines your destiny.'" Rick paused as if having an "aha moment" as he touched his finger to his chin. "When you think about it, Aristotle may have been alluding to another Serving Man, **Which**—a Seventh one. **Which** choice will I make?"

"Thank you for sharing that!" Rolly exclaimed. "And your comment afterward was most insightful." Rick nodded in thanks. "Believe it or not, I made that *choice* of excellence years ago, based on love."

"I believe that," Soni stated. She turned to address Rick. "I love that notion of a Seventh Serving Man. I will use that. '**Which** choice will I make?' could become another Key." Rick gave Soni a thumbs-up. "So, back to love, Rolly. I also love the second thing you did," she continued, referencing the third page. "You shared that you worked *with* them. I took the liberty of changing that to ***Play*** **With Them!** I hope that was okay."

"It's more than okay," Rolly confided. "It's what I *should* have said."

"Either way," Hal stated, "it felt like play to us."

Tiffany added, "The fact that he played *with* us is also significant. As Hal expressed earlier, we never felt we worked *for* Rolly. He wasn't in front of us, *leading*, or behind us, *managing*. He was beside us. He was *with* us, *helping*. He helped us grow. He helped us become *self*-managed."

"What a compliment," Soni stated. "Which leads me to the laminated definition of Empowerment. Although I work for and am paid by a corporation, my team must understand I'm relinquishing control over how someone in my position typically conducts business. I'm cutting the strings. I'm done with the role of a puppet master. They get the benefits of empowerment. They need to know they will now control their lives and claim their rights. They might ask why I'm willing to do this. It goes back to love. Karen shared that to empower someone *is* to love them. And in the business world, to empower others to become *self*-managed *is* the ultimate expression of love."

Rolly interjected, "Which leads you directly to the ***Self*-Management Model of Empowerment**—the laminated display on the table; it shows how you'll help make this happen."

"I hope it was all right that I added these pages, including Cheri's **Hall of Fame** at the end. I wanted to be able to display everyone's excellence in becoming *self*-managed."

"Soni, your willingness to 'bring something to the table' is the *only* way any of this continues to get better. I want to share these with my partners. It will become the latest enhancement to our ever-improving ***Self*-Management Program**. What we have just witnessed is precisely what happens when others feel empowered. We *all* will be thanking you for that."

"It was my privilege, sir. I'll text you the video I just took, which shows the order. So, have I earned the privilege of sharing more thoughts and asking a few questions?"

"Absolutely. Which will probably trigger questions and thoughts from us as well." Rolly smiled as he politely bowed. "Ladies first."

Horse First, Cart Second

Always the gentleman," Soni stated. "Let's begin with my current situation. Although I'm responsible for other departments—and I know with adjustments all I've learned will work for them as well—the immediate concern I posed to you and Ester was specific to sales. You may recall it was twofold. Neither my managers nor I have had any formal management training. In addition, our overall sales and profitability numbers have been decreasing. That said, it appears I have two *self*-management opportunities." She paused a moment to reconsider her answer. "Allow me to correct that. Rolly, there are three."

"Okay. And those would be?"

"The obvious two are my sales managers *and* my salespeople."

"I would agree," Rolly answered. "And the third?"

"*My* boss. *My* manager," Soni responded. "I need to walk Holly through everything I've learned to make certain she's comfortable with me *self*-managing myself without her in my mirrors. I'll thoroughly cover each document in hopes of receiving her blessing."

"Knowing she gave you her blessing to experience what you've been through this week, I'm certain you will receive it."

"I'm confident I will, too, Rolly. Come to think of it, she will likely want to share all this with *her* boss, who may want to do the same with *his*."

"That's how it works, Soni, when one sees the benefits of everyone becoming *self*-managed. So, back to your sales managers *and* your salespeople. Where do you begin?"

"I think it best I start with my managers. Since both are in the same boat, so to speak, I hope I can guide them through this together. Does that make sense?"

"It does," Rolly answered. "It will become a '*we*' experience where they may be able to help each other as both go about helping their teams."

"That's what I was hoping. As for what's on these tables, I foresee following the order I've laid out here. However, as I teach them how to learn and apply it with their team, I will also have them experience it firsthand. Am I on the right track?"

Rolly addressed Hal. "Since you've experienced this in your current position, I will ask for your input."

"Yes, ma'am, Soni," Hal answered. "*Their* end in mind is how they will apply it with their salespeople. Their *immediate* focus rests on how it applies to them. I'm sure you appreciate that some of these documents won't apply to their discipline, just like it wouldn't apply to yours when you meet with Holly." Hal pointed to several. "For example, PILLARS is not applicable, nor is MAINTENANCE. And the sales numbers for Goal Setting are derived from the numbers collected from their salespeople. Are you with me?"

"Yes, sir, Hal. Thank you."

"You're welcome. The documents we gave you today will be specific to their role in helping their salespeople. As for *their* role, with your help, they will list all the tasks *they* are responsible for executing on the TASK LIST document. Then you and they will spell out the REQUIREMENTS and EXPECTATIONS of those tasks on the next."

Soni rushed to the round table and returned with the tricycle. "I expect we will use the tricycle from the TASK REPORT CARD for each task," as she proudly held it up. "Correct?"

Tiffany answered, "Correct, Soni. You seem to like that little toy, don't you?"

"I *love* it, Tiffany. It reminds me of you and your story. It's the cutest thing ever—just like you."

Tiffany blushed. "You might be pleased to know that this 'cutest thing ever' will be returning to Texas with you. The tricycle," she clarified. "Not me. It's our little gift."

Soni grinned from ear to ear as she clutched it in her arms. "I will forever treasure this. Thank you all so very, *very* much!" Rick offered a wink.

Hal did, too. "You are most welcome, Soni. So, back to our task at hand."

Soni continued, "We will then use the TASK CLASSROOM ASSIGNMENT document to determine the classroom they will be assigned to with each task, which will identify my role, if needed, in helping them. It would also specify how frequently I would ***Be Present***, my level of ***Involvement***, and the amount of ***Time*** I would spend with them—if I'm in their mirrors at all."

"You got it. And because this is new to your people, they will likely want you in those mirrors at the beginning. And the EMPOWERMENT REVIEW SESSIONS document would need to be modified to fit their specific situation. Did this help?"

"Big time, Hal."

"Oh, there's one other thing you might want to change, Soni . . . their title. Our 'VPs of Sales' now proudly refer to themselves as 'VPs of Sales & *Self*-Management.' They are *self*-managing themselves while helping their salespeople become *self*-managed."

"Boy, do I love that!" Soni exclaimed. "We can rename our 'Sales Managers,' too. We can proudly refer to them as '*Self*-Managers'—a title more worthy of their immense responsibility."

"Most appropriate adjustments for both of you," Rolly affirmed. So, what's the next step for you and your *self*-managers, Soni?"

Introducing the Plan

Once I've guided my managers through the plan, which shouldn't take more than a couple of days at best, we will be ready to introduce it to their teams. Given the stark change from the way our salespeople have been managed, I don't see this being shared individually. It allows misinformation to spread from one to another. Instead, bringing all our salespeople together to receive a 'big picture' overview of this new *opportunity* would be wiser. It might take on the feel of the first meeting you had with your team, Rolly."

"I'm with you, Soni. And what would you focus on?"

Soni referenced the first table. "Everything I've laid out up to, and including, the ***Self*-Management Model of Empowerment**. Come to think of it, we might even incorporate a little history lesson to add some spice. Rudyard Kipling's 1902 poem might prove of interest. Even more so is the discussion I had with Karen and Vicky that connected this model to our nation's fight for independence, including the selfie Karen took of us at Gadsby's."

"I think that would add great impact, Soni. You might also include your experience visiting Ester and Rob's gym. Your people can likely relate to someone *deciding* to improve their health and fitness as compared to actually *doing* something about it."

"Thank you for that reminder. I'm not *deciding* to include it . . . I'm *doing* it! I may even ask them about the three frogs on the log." Everyone smiled.

"And who do you see leading this discussion?"

"If my *self*-managers are comfortable doing it, that's likely my preference. Yet, due to my involvement with everyone these past few days, they might prefer *I* handle at least part of it. I'll empower them to make the decision."

"Oh, I like that," Rolly exclaimed. "Once done, how do you see rolling this out? Who do you begin with first?"

Executing the Plan

We'll have to look at the numbers. Let me explain," Soni surmised. "It will take several visits, each lasting up to one to two hours, which will occur over a two- to three-week period. We're talking about three or four appointments per day, per *self*-manager with their people. Then we'll plug in the number of salespeople each one has, which will tell us how many appointments we can make per week. Once we know that number, we should have a sign-up list for after the meeting to see who wants to be first."

Rick smiled. "That's essentially how Rolly discovered who wanted help the most from his team. Which we all know turned out to be me. I see this approach accomplishing two things: First, it will tell you who's most excited—where your early successes will be. Second, it will tell you who's most reluctant—where your greatest challenges might occur. That's helpful to know."

Rolly asked, "Can I anticipate the few salespeople you've already identified as being *self*-managed, whose *Gauges* and *Warning Lights* are doing fine, are expected to be on that list?"

"Without question. Everyone must be on it. And anyone whom we determine is in the *Front Row* of *Senior Classroom A* on the TASKS they are expected to have mastered won't get much of our time and attention."

"As it should be," Tiffany agreed. "One more question, Soni. What is your plan when someone new is brought on board with no experience?" Her subtle wink reminded Soni how far Tiffany had come after starting with no experience in new home sales.

Soni smiled and pointed to the four tables. "We will expose them to *everything*. The Six Keys and the doors opened by our Six Serving Men that leads them to become *self*-managed and empowered."

"The fact that you will create an *entire* team of *self*-managed individuals will afford you the luxury of having time to do just that. All of which frees you up to invest additional time in looking out for their success and well-being," Tiffany emphasized.

Freeing Others Frees Us

That's a valid point, Tiffany. I fully expect to realize many benefits for them, *and* us, in everyone becoming *self*-managed."

Hal responded, "Soni, we've discussed the fact that when you empower your people to set their own goals, they almost always set them higher than what the company's business plan dictates. More sales is always a good thing. We can shift our attention to a ton of worthwhile things when we're not worried about them making sales."

"I can appreciate that, Hal."

Rick interjected, "Speaking of appreciation, people who feel valued and appreciated, and are treated with dignity and respect, tend to stay where they are. Which means the high rate of turnover so prevalent in our industry is significantly reduced. Having a loyal team takes a lot of worry and pressure off us."

Soni sighed, "That's a relief, for sure, Rick. I hadn't thought of that."

Hal added, "As for your *self*-managers, for every person on their team who becomes *self*-managed, *they* are now free to do other things that bring value to them, the team, and the organization. Like analyze what's happening in the marketplace: assessing how their neighborhoods, amenities, floorplans, pricing, quality of homes, and the buying experiences they create compare to their competition."

"That's big, Hal."

Tiffany pointed to the tricycle Soni was still holding. "Or, free to search for and integrate new books, fresh ideas, and inspiring educational programs into the culture of the team, just like what you're doing right now! Resources, Soni, that further develop their knowledge and skills . . . that enhance their positive attitude and willingness to take direction . . . and reinforce the values and principles that embody who they are."

"Enrich the mind and the spirit. Oh, that's goooood, Tiffany! Thank you." Soni held up the tricycle. "I've got one to add. Or, free to seek out, identify, and interview the right candidates that can pass the 'tricycle test'—so we don't miss out on great experienced talent or *new* talent like the Kelly Youngs, the Tiffany Torgans, and the Hal Looneys of the world."

Rick smiled, "When we empower others, when we give them the freedom to control *their* life and claim *their* rights, they give us something in return—*our* freedom."

Rolly spoke up, "And that freedom is worth its weight in gold!"

"Or, Goldfish," Soni added with a grin. Everyone chuckled, especially Rolly!

"Very good everyone. Soni, do you have any further questions for us?"

Share the Love

I really don't," she didn't hesitate. "Yet I do have something to share. Once I get the ball rolling with my *self*-managers and their teams, I intend to contact my counterparts at the other divisions within our company. I must get them to enroll in the next available ***Self*-Management Retreat**. I must help them recognize the value in investing in themselves *and* their teams. This isn't an option. It's a must!"

"I'm pleased to know you feel that strongly about this."

"I do. I want to help them empower their people to become *self*-managed. I want to help them cut the strings they're pulling, which ironically are the very things holding them back. I want them and their people to enjoy more success *and* experience a higher quality of life. There's a better way to do what we do, and I know it now. And until they get in a class, I will share with them as much of what I've experienced this week as I can." Soni pointed to Rick, Tiffany, and Hal. "And just like what happened with these three, I know when the student becomes the teacher, I, too, will grow in my understanding of its power."

Rick agreed, "We can assure you it *will* happen." Tiffany and Hal nodded.

"I also intend to share this experience with my friends. Everyone needs this. Professionally, whether employed or self-employed. In any profession. At any level. No matter what the industry, they can benefit by becoming *self*-managed. And in their personal lives, I'm confident this will also make a difference. Often people try to do things to make their life better, yet fall short; they fail to make it happen. I have a good feeling that when we help them become *self*-managed, the excitement of turning failures into successes will follow."

A Sobering Thought

You don't know the half of it, Soni," Hal responded as he motioned to his feathered friend. "You might be interested to learn what Rolly just shared with us regarding how this ***Self*-Management Model** is helping those battling addiction."

"Addiction?" Soni quizzed, pleasantly surprised. "I'd *love* to hear more. I can't imagine anything more meaningful or timely in today's society. I have a friend battling alcohol addiction. It's serious. We're talking more stints in rehab than one would care to mention. Quite frankly, he's fortunate to still be alive. He's attended rehab with many who are not."

Rick interjected, "I have friends and family who have dealt with addiction, and the statistics are alarming, Soni. In the U.S. alone, approximately 178,000 people die from excessive drinking each year. That's almost five hundred people . . . *every*

. . . *single* . . . *day!* And for those unfortunate souls, it has shortened their lives by an average of twenty-four years, one-third of the average lifespan!"[15]

Rolly spoke up, "Soni, before we came in, I was sharing that I'm close friends with a dear couple, Kristine Ehrlich and Montana Harris, who have experienced their share of heartache and misery with addiction. She with alcohol. He, alcohol and heroin. I've learned a great deal from them. They have learned from their reading and treatments that an addict is best described as an actor who wants to direct the entire performance—the set, lights, actors, dancers, *everything.* But when the show doesn't go well, they blame everyone else."

Tiffany spoke up, "That sounds like a control issue."

"Exactly," Rolly answered. "Kristine further elaborated . . . 'Even when we're trying to be kind,' she said, 'we're still self-seeking. Even when trying to be honest, we're still ego driven. Even in our *best* moments, we're usually causing confusion rather than harmony. It's tough on us, but it may be tougher on our families! We *want* to be *self*-managed. But *self*-management isn't possible in our lives until we're willing to do *one* thing . . . stop playing God.' Montana added that, early on, addicts have zero concept of accountability. He said, either we never learned it, it was stolen from us by trauma, or it atrophied through addiction."

"That's got to be gut-wrenching to deal with," Soni admitted. "I'm curious what you shared with Kristine and Montana regarding the ***Self*-Management Model** that is helping those battling addiction. I can definitely see the Six Keys and their Serving Men being a fit."

---

[15] www.cdc.gov/alcohol/facts-stats/index.html

"They did, too, Soni. But what resonated with them most was the mirrors on the two walls. From their perspective, that analogy was beautiful, powerful, and symbolic."

"How so?" Soni inquired.

"They stated that *before* recovery, the addict doesn't see their reflection in the mirror. They see a mask. A mask made of trauma, survival, shame, guilt, self-deception, denial, and fear. As a result, an addict won't ask for help when they don't even recognize themselves in the mirror. Being *unrecognizable* corresponds with their life being *unmanageable*."

"Everything must seem in disarray, Rolly."

"Precisely. They added that until the addict sees that they cannot do this alone . . . until they accept that they need God and people they can trust to help them and hold them accountable, and are willing to *share* that *control* with them—to be in their mirrors—do they have any chance at recovery."

"That's profound, Rolly. What a *huge* breakthrough!"

"It is, Soni. I'm pleased to share that these two are using this model at the sober living house Montana runs. He's even hung mirrors in the hallways to serve as a reminder of the help and accountability that is *always* there . . . for *everyone*! Moved to tears, the two stated that this model, and these mirrors, are truly a Godsend. These tools are making a difference in the lives of others who *deserve* a different life! And that's not just the addict. It includes family and loved ones as well."

A Masterpiece in the Making

For once, I'm at a total loss for words," Soni confessed as she wiped tears from her eyes. The others followed suit.

"The very first call I'll make when I return home will be to my friend. I'm beyond excited to introduce him to the ***Self-*** **Management Model** and the mirrors! I'm praying it will help him."

Rick interjected, "And I'll be doing the same with my friends and family."

Soni paused to reflect. "Rolly, I'm guessing that when you began working on this idea of *self*-management, you recognized it had the potential to save *careers.* But I'm betting you didn't foresee it having the potential to save *lives.*"

"You're correct. That was never part of the original vision. But I've learned when you give life to an idea, it often takes on a life of its own. Who knows? Perhaps *it* felt empowered. This much I do know. I can only take credit for the idea. What has evolved, what has been created and shared, is a labor of love from everyone you've met with this week."

"Again, Rolly, I love your humility." Soni opened her arms wide to symbolically take in all four tables. "It's important all of you know that in *my* humble opinion, what has been created here as a result of the contribution *everyone* has made is nothing short of brilliant!"

Hal smiled. "A most appropriate choice of words, Soni. Years ago, before the three of us moved on to other opportunities, Rolly gave us two parting gifts. I would expect we all still have both."

"Don't tell me one was a tricycle," Soni responded as she proudly held hers up.

Tiffany responded, "Good guess, Soni! That was the first one. The second was a framed picture of the most magnificent, beautifully colored butterflies you've ever seen."

Rick added, "They were to signify a new beginning. Change. A metamorphosis. And an opportunity to grow wings and soar to new heights. As gorgeous as the picture was, the message engraved at the bottom is what moved us most."

"Do any of you recall that message?" Soni inquired.

Hal spoke up, "It *happens* to be my screensaver." He touched the screen on his phone to display it. The word **BRILLIANCE** prominently appeared in large letters just under the collection of butterflies. The message was revealed below it. "You're welcome to read it aloud, Soni."

She cleared her throat . . .

"WHEN A COLLECTION OF BRILLIANT MINDS, HEARTS, AND TALENTS COME TOGETHER . . . EXPECT A MASTERPIECE"

She continued. "*This* is brilliant! The message is *so* true. What everyone has helped create here *is* a masterpiece. I would have treasured and kept this gift, too!"

Tiffany reached for her handbag she had placed under the round table earlier. From it she retrieved a newly wrapped gift and offered it to Soni. "Since you're now one of us, and have your own tricycle just like us, we felt it appropriate you should have this, too."

Soni quickly unwrapped it to find the same picture Hal just showed her. It was beautifully framed. Best of all, it was signed by the four of them. She was visibly moved as she choked back tears. "How can I *ever* thank all of you? This week has been incredible! Sunday afternoon, I found myself on a stage at the gym. Now I find myself on another stage. Is someone trying to tell me something?"

Rolly spread his wings. "Perhaps the stage has been set for a new beginning. An *opportunity* . . ." He paused and winked at Soni before starting over. "An *opportunity* for you to spread *your* wings and soar to new heights on a most fulfilling journey to *self*-management." Everyone cheered, hugged, and smiled!

It was time to move their celebration outside. Hal suggested everyone join Soni's family poolside, where drinks and hors d'oeuvres would be served. He would bring Soni's carry-on.

Soni volunteered to escort Rolly and bring the Goldfish for snacking. She was beyond excited to see her family and introduce them to everyone!

Tiffany offered to insert the pages from the tables into Soni's binder. She would bring it, the laminated display, Soni's handbag, the tricycle, and the framed, autographed picture.

Rick offered to help the staff clear the stage.

It had been a remarkable day for Soni. In truth, it had been a remarkable week. And there was more to come. Another limo ride would take everyone to dinner, where the celebration continued in the Library Room at Dominick's Steakhouse in North Scottsdale. Soni would meet Shellie, Rick's wife, and Rachel, Hal's wife. Bill, Tiffany's husband, flew in from a business trip to join in the festivities. Kelly and her husband, Rick, would also be there. And David Osborn, Rolly's friend from Austin, joined them, too.

The highlight of the evening was a surprise Zoom call displayed on a big screen. Soni would get to speak with everyone she had met during the week. Holly was also on the call. The energy proved electrifying.

The next morning, everyone, including spouses, enjoyed a round of golf at another of Hal's magnificent communities nestled within the Mazatzal Mountains and Tonto National Forest.

When they wrapped up, the entire group left with monogrammed shirts and blouses, compliments of their host. Following lunch, Rolly, David, Soni, and her family were whisked away to the airport to return to Texas. It was an emotional goodbye for all.

Yes, life *has* been good to Soni Graves. And life is about to get better for all who know and love her. She is empowered. And she will *manage* to put lots of smiles on lots of faces. Correct that. She will *self*-manage to put lots of smiles on lots of faces. What an *opportunity!*

Acknowledgments

If I've said this once, I've said it a thousand times: everyone I meet is here to teach me something. Which means . . . everyone I have met has helped mold me into who I am and what I know. Which means . . . in some way, shape, form, or fashion, they have all made a contribution to this book. Which means . . . I owe *everyone* who has ever crossed my path a big THANK YOU! So, there it is.

And thanks to this book, I now have an entire *new* list of folks whom I wrote about to also thank. To them, I wish to express my deepest gratitude for the willingness of so many to bare their souls—that's the best way I know to describe it—for what they gave me permission to reveal about their lives. They didn't have to disclose their struggles and tragedies, but they did it anyway. And I love them for it. It's what makes us human. Now that you've completed this book, my hope is that you felt as personally connected with them as a reader as I did as a writer.

Not included in the storyline, but found in the Advance Praise section at the beginning of the book, are Rodney Hall, Ken Pinto, and Karen Steinmann, who deserve a special thank you.

Rodney, President of Rodney Hall Executive Search, is the reason my wife, Susan, and I founded our consulting firm twenty years ago. We thank him for that *push* we both needed. And since Rodney knows everybody and their brother in homebuilding and real estate—and loves connecting people—he knew I needed to meet Ken Pinto. So, he made it happen.

Ken is a homebuilding veteran and author of *How Much Is the Milk?* and my counterpart in homebuilding. With construction expertise running through his veins, Ken runs an international supply chain solutions company. He trains builders and suppliers in how to work together to lower each other's costs—thus helping both home ownership and the industry to thrive. Since our meeting, our firms have formed a strategic alliance. Ken refers clients our way who need sales and *self*-management help. We refer ours his way who need help with construction and cost savings. It's a win-win for him, for us, and for the companies we both have the privilege of serving. Like Rodney, Ken is also a connector and referred us to Karen Steinmann.

Karen's expertise is editing. She edited Ken's book. Based on that introduction and his strong recommendation, I asked Karen to edit this one. I admire her patience, persistence, and genuine love for the written word. Her challenge was to make an uncultured redneck *sound* semi-intelligent—a daunting task, for sure. I'm grateful she accepted my request.

An extra-special thank you is extended to Rita Ramirez. Rita is the owner of Sonrisa Photography. Her job was to make me *look* semi-intelligent—another formidable endeavor. She took the photo you see on the back cover and the photos you will see when you check out our NewWings Consulting website to learn more about what our team does.

And how did I find Rita? Soni Graves connected us. Rita and Soni attended college together.

Scott Andrew James is another name worth noting. Scott is the VP of Author Strategies at Pioneering Collective. He provided guidance with the publishing of this book. In addition to that expertise, Scott is a typewriter poet. He creates poems live and in person on his 1946 Smith-Corona typewriter. He is also the author of three books of poetry, and an accomplished speaker. He's one cool dude!

As always, I must pay tribute to my family. My grandfather, Travis Bracewell, taught me the value of putting people first and having fun in everything you do. My parents, E.C. and Bobbie Rigby, taught me manners, values, and the importance of doing things right—the first time. I also got my work ethic from them. In the words of my songwriting mentor and cowriter, Richard Leigh, "Everything they gave me, took all they had." My siblings—David, Laura, Paul, and Lynda—made me want to become a better brother. My children—Tammy, Tracy, Clint, Courtney, Brock, and Brooke—helped me, and still are helping me, become a better father. My sons-in-law—Michael and Rayne—are helping me become a better father-in-law. My grandchildren—Elizabeth, Melody, Kaitlyn, Caroline, Kendall, and Camille—are teaching me how to spoil them. And now I can add *great* grandchildren to that list: Adrian and Claire. And last, but certainly not least, my bride of twenty-eight years and counting: my princess, Susan. She's helping me become the man she deserves: her prince. I make certain she wakes up every morning with a fresh cup of coffee at her bedside. I've got a long way to go, but I'm told I'm making progress!

Resources for *Managing* to S.M.I.L.E.

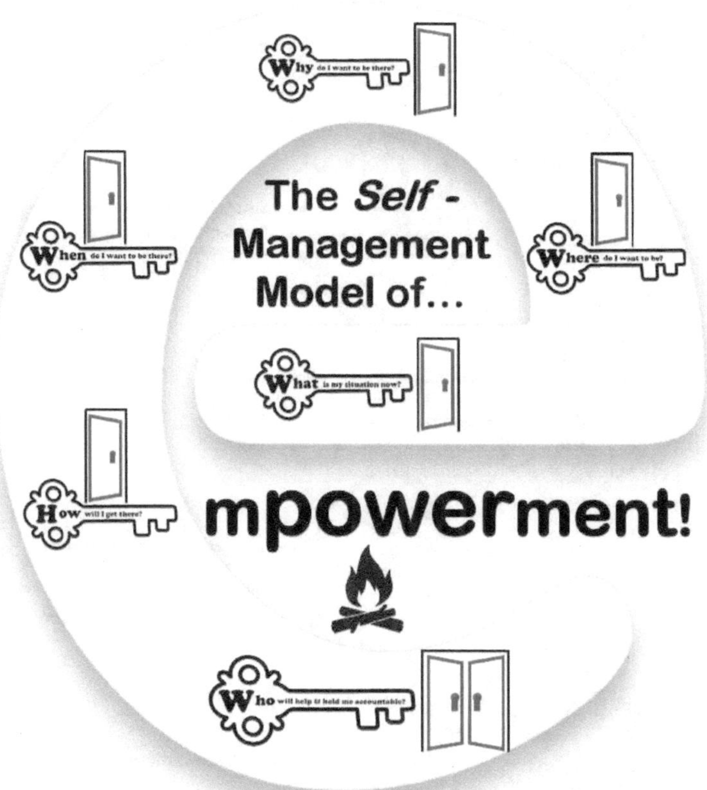

Six Keys to *Self*-Management

The Seventh Key to *Self*-Management

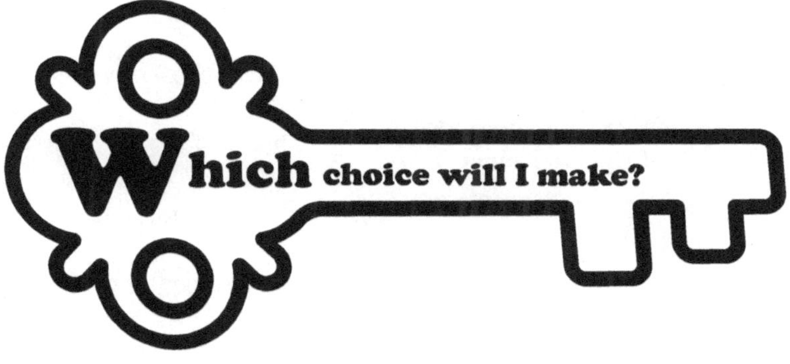

Soni's Order to *Self*-Management

1	**Blend Success in Business with Quality of Life**	18	Image of the **Where** Key
2	**Create a Culture of Excellence!**	19	**WHERE** DO I WANT TO BE AND **WHEN?**
3	SIX PERSONAL PERSPECTIVES	20	LIFE GOALS
4	***Play* <u>With</u> Them!**	21	CAST YOUR VISION
5	Definition of **Empowerment**	22	NON-NEGOTIABLES
6	***Self*-Management Model of Empowerment**	23	Image of the **Why** Key
7	I KEEP SIX HONEST SERVING MEN	24	YOUR BIG LIFE
8	Image of the **What** Key	25	YOUR VALUE PROPOSITION
9	**WHAT** IS MY SITUATION NOW?	26	Image of the **When** Key
10	PAST-YEAR BUSINESS REVIEW	27	GOALS FOR REALISTIC ACHIEVERS
11	PILLARS	28	GOALS FOR BIG DREAMERS
12	MAINTENANCE	29	Image of the **How** Key
13	FOUR LAWS OF A DATABASE	30	Image of the **Who** Key
14	STRUGGLES	31	TASK CLASSROOM ASSIGNMENT
15	TASK LIST	32	CHOOSE AN ACCOUNT-ABILITY PARTNER
16	TASK REQUIREMENTS & EXPECTATIONS	33	EMPOWERMENT REVIEW SESSIONS
17	TASK REPORT CARD	34	**Hall of Fame**

www.ingramcontent.com/pod-product-compliance
Lightning Source LLC
LaVergne TN
LVHW100522110826
845146LV00002B/738

9798218914998